Living, Sleeping and Eating
♫ *Band* ♫

My Memoirs of Marching Band

Michele L. Mathews

PublishAmerica
Baltimore

First printing

ISBN: 1-4137-8326-0
PUBLISHED BY PUBLISHAMERICA, LLLP
www.publishamerica.com
Baltimore

Printed in the United States of America

For Frank Cedar Battaglia –
Without you,
The rest of the staff,
and that awesome band,
I never would have made it
through my rough times.
You are a great teacher,
mentor,
and friend.

Acknowledgments

A huge thanks goes to my children, Ashley and Jonathan "Jonny" Fender, for putting up with me while I worked on this book, my parents Mike and Sharon Mathews for driving me to all of my band functions and being chaperones, and my brother Sean Mathews for being dragged to my band functions.

I want to thank all of the band directors who made my band memories so memorable: Norris Houston, Chris Cinnamon, Pete Vogler, Mark McHenry, Richard Coomer, Rick Heacock, Jerry Vogel, and Frank Battaglia.

Thanks to PublishAmerica for giving me the opportunity to become a published writer and making my dream come true.

I thank each and every person who touched my life in some form or another during my nearly 15 years of band. Without you, this book could not have been written.

A very special thanks to God for leading me to the local newspaper online and to an article about an author who is also getting published at PublishAmerica. That article directed me to PublishAmerica's web site. If I hadn't discovered that article, this book would probably have never been published.

♫

Chapter 1

"You guys between Lisa and Amy need to make sure you keep your horns to the box," the staff member working with the clarinets said. "The judges need to hear this part."

They all looked at the young college woman as though they understood the instructions.

"I have a question," Natalie asked.

"What's your question?" the woman asked.

"How many counts is our next move?" she asked.

"Twenty-four," the woman replied, looking at the next drill chart.

That staff member was me as an Indiana University senior during my first week as a marching instructor for the Martinsville Marching Artesians, a band I had been a part of as a high school student, and a band that meant a lot to me afterward. When I became a clarinet player in the sixth grade, I never dreamed band would become such a huge part of my life; I also never dreamed I would become a staff member for one of the Top 10 Class A bands in Indiana.

In order to understand how important marching band became to me, I think it is important to know the ups and downs of my years as a band student. I don't remember why I even decided to be in band. Maybe my decision was based on my need to belong, and since I wasn't athletically inclined, band became the best extra-curricular activity for me. Another possible reason for joining band might have been my father's influence, because he was a drummer when he was in band. In fact, my father's band director was my sixth grade band director, Mr. Robert Austin.

Deciding on an instrument to play proved to be fairly difficult. Mr. Austin talked me out of playing the instrument I thought I wanted to learn, the trumpet. He told my mother that since I would be obtaining a metal mouth I should learn an instrument like the flute or clarinet. Braces would cause me problems on an instrument like a trumpet, he told my mother. I chose the clarinet.

Instead of spending enormous bucks on a new clarinet, my parents bought me a used plastic one, as opposed to wood, for $75. The clarinet needed some repair work, new pads and corks, costing around $100. I had really wanted a new one, but if I wasn't sure about staying in band, my parents wouldn't lose as much money. I couldn't blame them.

I can't remember Mr. Austin very well; I only had him for that one year because we moved from Huntington, Indiana, to Kokomo, Indiana, the summer after I finished the sixth grade. I do remember Mr. Austin calling me Michael many repeated times; Michael was my father's first name. The similarities in our first names confused him, and he wasn't the only one who had called me Michael. I also recall him telling my mother I was the best clarinet player out of the six he had. A compliment like that one made me feel great, especially since I wasn't even sure about being in band.

Our first and only concert happened on May 14, 1981, and the whole school, Andrews Elementary, was involved. Each grade level, including the two kindergarten classes, sang songs to a small gymnasium full of parents, grandparents, siblings, and other assorted relatives. The sixth grade band consisting of two flutes, six clarinets, two alto saxophones, two trumpets, and one drummer performed first on the wooden stage set up just for the concert.

The butterflies fluttered wildly in my stomach as the 13 of us prepared to play in front of a standing-room-only crowd for the first time. To say I was nervous was an understatement. I can't begin to say what I was feeling at the moment I walked up the wooden stage stairs hoping I didn't fall on my nose and embarrass myself. I also kept hoping I didn't forget how to finger the notes or how to blow through the instrument making the notes. I sat in the front row on the end and felt as though everyone's brown, blue, or whatever color, eyes were on me. I tried not to so much as even glance at the audience and instead focused my dark brown eyes on either Mr. Austin or my music stand.

Our part of the concert wasn't as bad as I thought it would be. In fact, Mr. Austin seemed pleased with our performance. Mr. Austin made all 13 of us stand as we received applause. I was so relieved we were finished that I did not think about those eyes staring at me. I even managed a smile.

I don't have many memories of my sixth grade band, but what memories I do have are treasured as my first year of band, the year I was undecided about being in band.

Becoming a seventh grade band student wasn't going to be as easy as being a sixth grade band student. During the week after school let out for summer vacation, I subjected myself to the first exposure of marching band.

My mother had already bought me a pair of marching shoes two weeks before the marching band practices began. Buying the shoes must have been my excitement shining through because I was a nervous wreck on Monday, June 1, 1981, the first day of practice. I wasn't brave enough to sit in the front row like I had as a sixth grader. Besides, I felt the eighth and ninth graders deserved those seats since they were older and had been in band longer than me. The bald-headed band director, Mr. Charles Glover, was intimidating to me.

The practices were horrible, or at least for me they were. I disliked being there, because I didn't know anyone. In fact, I didn't know any of the other clarinet players. My fellow sixth grade classmates had all quit. I'm not sure if any of the 13 had even stayed in band, except the drummer, and I ignored him.

We had to memorize a song called "Reach Out." That song was being used for an AT & T commercial so having to play and march to it made me feel like the walking commercial. I had difficulty learning and marching to the song. I didn't believe my brain, arms, and legs were coordinated that well because they wouldn't function together and turn me into a marching professional, not that I expected that to happen right away.

Just when I thought I knew the song well enough, we would go outside to practice marching around the school, and I couldn't play and march at the same time. The whole situation frustrated me because I knew I should be able to do this. I had to learn, otherwise I would make a fool of myself during the parades, the Huntington Heritage Days, and the North Webster Mermaid Festival, in which we were to participate. I couldn't and absolutely refused to make a fool of myself in front of my hometown crowd and in front of both sets of grandparents, who had lake cottages on Webster Lake.

Helping in my decision to quit summer marching band was a little voice saying, "Michele, your family is moving 60 miles away. Why bother getting to know the other band members and learning to march when you will only be here to the end of June?" (My father worked for an electric company and was transferred.)

I listened to that voice and decided not to march as a Riverview Junior High Marching Raider. I mean, what was the point? Well, I would have learned the fundamentals of marching but then again Mr. Glover, who was my band director for exactly three days, really wasn't even doing that. He put us in lines, told us when to start moving, when our instruments were to come up, and yelled at us if we weren't marching on the correct foot. So, the only reason for me to stay was the yelling I would receive because I wasn't coordinated enough. I never saw any of the band students or their bald-headed director again.

In August 1981, I became a student of the Kokomo-Center Consolidated School Corporation by beginning at Maple Crest Middle School. They didn't have a marching band at this level, so I didn't have to worry about my coordination problem until I became a freshman in high school. In the meantime, the assistant director at the high school, Mr. Travis Murray, was my director at Maple Crest so I acquainted myself with him since I would be around him for the next six years. Mr. Murray was younger than either Mr. Austin or

Mr. Glover; I would guess he was probably late 20s or early 30s, not a father figure to his students by any means.

As with my sixth grade year, I don't really remember much about my two middle school years. Part of the reason might be because I didn't take band as seriously as I should have. I had a tough time adjusting at the middle school level, especially at Maple Crest. Not only was I the new kid on the block, but I soon realized I really wasn't as good as what I was led to believe. Instead of sitting on the front row and playing the first parts, I sat on the third row and played third parts. This band, consisting of seventh and eighth graders, had more clarinets than my whole sixth grade band had members.

Like I have already stated, I don't remember much about my seventh grade year. A couple of months, actually, November, Mr. Murray yelled at me for either playing a wrong note or playing a note at the wrong time. I had never had a teacher yell at me before so naturally I was upset. I was an honor roll student who was never a discipline problem. In fact, I was so quiet I didn't know how he even remembered I was there in his class. I wasn't much of a talker, especially since I was in a new school and didn't know anyone that well yet.

On the other hand, Mr. M, as we called him sometimes, could be a really fun teacher when he wanted to be. A few weeks after he yelled at me, we had a jazz band perform during band class. The group played a song called "Salted Peanuts," and as the song was played, Mr. M seemed to think he should teach us the words so he sang along. He wasn't very much of a singer, which made the situation even funnier.

A pay telephone, located in the lobby area outside the small auditorium, received constant usage from Mr. M. When he wasn't in the auditorium where band met, he could always be found with the receiver stuck to his ear. He wasn't married, but he could have been talking to his girlfriend, providing he had one. Anyway, Mr. M always managed a wave or even a smile if I happened to see him standing there using the phone.

After Christmas break, he had us play a game with the 12 major scales we had to memorize and be able to play in a minute or less with no mistakes. Mr. M had one student pick a number between 1 and 38, the number of students in class. The student picked 35. Then he told me to choose a number between 1 and 10, and I picked 2. Using his grade book where our names each had a number beside it, he went up 2 to 33; my name was number 33. I had to play the last four scales, the hardest four scales to learn.

Our last concert of the school year was the last week in May. The seventh and eighth grade band had already performed, and most of us sat in the back of the auditorium and watched the jazz band perform their songs. During a break in their performance, one member gave Mr. M a huge box. In front of a good-sized crowd, he opened the box only to find a smaller box inside.

"Oh, my," he commented. He opened the smaller box to discover a gift certificate from a local department store.

He walked to the front of the jazz band where he spoke into the microphone, "Now we'll go on."

By the time I was in the eighth grade, I had become a very loyal and dedicated Rick Springfield fan. I owned everything I could find either written, photographed, or both about him including albums, magazines, and other assorted memorabilia. Mr. M wasn't very fond of Rick and was always giving me a bad time about liking him.

Right before Christmas break, at the beginning of class, one incident about my idolizing of Rick and Mr. M sticks out in my mind the most. I had worn my "I Love Rick Springfield" button to school that day, an item I wore almost every day. After reading the button, Mr. M started teasing me about the button. He asked another clarinet player what she thought of Rick, and she agreed with me. Mr. M continued this conversation by saying how disgusting Rick looks when he sings at concerts, how sweaty he gets, and how he wears cut-off shirts and gloves with the finger tips cut off. We had to move to the choir room a few minutes after class began because the choir had to practice for a concert. In the choir room the director had put up several posters of Rick. The clarinet player called Mr. M's attention to the posters, and he said Rick looked cute in those.

General Hospital, the soap opera Rick was on, became the topic of conversation several times in band. Of course, we weren't supposed to even be talking, but we sometimes did anyway. I sat between two other third part clarinets. Anyway, Alexa and the newest band member discussed one particular incident from the show, a scene in which Rick's character, Dr. Noah Drake, got slapped by a woman. The scene was absolutely hysterical, but I guess you had to see it.

I wish I could remember more about my early years in band, but as I have already stated, band didn't mean that much to me until my four years in high school when marching band changed my life for the better, or at least I believe it did.

♫

Chapter 2

If someone asked me what the turning point was in my seven years of band, I believe I would have to say my freshman year. In fact, I almost did not even stay in band because my coordination problem continued its existence. I truly believed I would never be coordinated enough to march like one of the upperclassmen.

As a freshman at Haworth High School, one of two city high schools in Kokomo, one of the first items on the agenda for the 1983–1984 school year was a week away from home for band camp. On the first Sunday in August, I left behind my family, for the first time in 14 years, for Manchester College in North Manchester, Indiana. The week's memories vaguely stick in my mind. That Sunday was sunny and ridiculously hot, and no air conditioning could be found anywhere, not on the bus and not in the dormitory where we slept. To top it all off, the freshmen had to unload the equipment truck. I thought I would die from heat exhaustion.

On the first full day of camp, we spent most of it working on music and learning marching basics. I had so much trouble just trying to stay in step that it was not even close to being funny. The directors, Tom Haggard and Mr. Murray, didn't work with us individually or in small groups. I tried my best and listened to the upperclassmen's yelling. I really frustrated myself with this coordination problem, but what could I do? No one would help me. I had two choices. I either stuck it out or I quit. Even though I disliked band at this point, my second option wasn't really an option to me. One girl, who marched next to me in our show, had already quit. She had called her mother, who drove the hour to one and a half hours to the college to pick her up. Many of the students believed she quit because she didn't want to be initiated.

If that girl thought initiation would be bad, she was crazy. Initiation was the easy part. The girls had to dress in clashing clothes, have our hair put into ponytails and do whatever the senior girls asked us to do. Manchester College wouldn't allow shaving cream and other nasty stuff causing nasty messes so we lucked out in that department. Speaking of luck, the boys only had to wear leaves (with clothes under them) on a string around a certain part of their body, which shall remain nameless here, but I think you can probably guess. Within an hour, most of them had lost their leaves. However, the senior boys made them do a lot more, like pushups, than the senior girls did us, so I guess it all evened out in the end.

By the following Friday, we had learned most of the music and drill for our show. The freshmen had also added new words to our vocabulary, words pertaining to marching band. Mr. Haggard gave us red, white, and blue poker chips to mark our spots as we learned the drill. I didn't have too much trouble getting from one spot to another except for the fact I couldn't stay on the correct foot. Here again part of my trouble might have been the fact that I hadn't taken band as seriously as I should have. Many of the better musicians had taken private lessons, which I hadn't pushed Mom and Dad to let me do.

I was glad to be home on Friday. The week I had dreaded was done, and I had survived somehow miraculously. However, the band had one more week of camp at the high school, which was good. We had air conditioning for our lunch break, and we could go home to sleep in our own beds where I could actually get a good night's sleep. The second week of band camp wasn't much different than the first. We had two extra people to help teach us our show, Harold and Barb Gallant. Harold did the marching parts and also worked the guard's routine as did his wife. We continued learning and perfecting our approximately 10-minute show. The only excitement was a couple of seniors who decided to give one or two freshmen swirlies, which had been forbidden at college.

Once school began, the Marching Huskies' fall marching season began. We marched at the home varsity football games and practiced four days a week for the contests in which we would compete. Two of our practices were after school, and the other two were later in the evening. Our practices weren't usually too exciting. We either marched the show the way we were supposed to do or we didn't. If the show wasn't perfected like it was supposed to be, Mr. Haggard yelled at us and continued yelling until we did it right. Like any other "sport," we learned very quickly to do it right the first time. We, me, in particular, didn't want him yelling. I had already been yelled at enough, and it was time to stop. Don't get me wrong. Mr. Haggard could be really cool when he wanted to be. He was a little on the chubby side, like Mr. Murray, married, and probably in his 30s. He could tell some pretty funny statements or jokes when he was in a good mood. His reddish-colored hair told you what kind of a temper he had, and the hair didn't lie.

On September 17, 1983, our first contest happened at Winchester High School. All 101 of us, including 22 in color guard and 12 in percussion, performed our show at 1:36 P.M. Our senior drum major led us onto the field where we performed "Antiphon," "Eli's Coming," and "Music/The Endless Enigma." The music was pretty tough for me because some of the notes were above the staff, and I had never played those notes before. All I could do was try my best and then know or learn what I had to do to make my part in the show better, which turned out to be quite a bit. I had trouble with the counts and didn't march on the correct foot, as usual. I even tried what the clarinet section leader suggested. I didn't play part of the time; instead, I counted each move, which helped somewhat. At this contest the band received a score but no placing. Mr. Haggard had decided to have us do this contest as an exhibition meaning we really didn't compete. We only received a score.

Our own contest, the Haworth Invitational, was another one of those exhibition performances. Since we were the contest host, we couldn't compete for that fine first place trophy. That was something you just didn't do in the marching band world. In fact, we didn't receive anything except a score. Just like the Indiana State School Music Association (ISSMA) contests, our invitational had four classes, A, B, C, and D, and was based upon school enrollment of the previous year for grades 10–12. The winners that particular year included Anderson Highland – Class A, Lawrence North – Class B, Western – Class C, and Lewis Cass – Class D. Of course, these winners could change every year depending upon each school's enrollment; some schools, because their enrollment is close to the cut-off point, change back and forth from one class to another and then back again.

The ISSMA District contest at Lewis Cass High School was the most important of the season. If we didn't receive a certain score and a Division I, we didn't advance to the regional contest. As a Class B band performing at 3:17 P.M., we earned a Division I rating and advanced to regional at our own Haworth High School two weeks later. Eight schools around Indiana hosted approximately 200 bands in all four classes at the district level. Not only did we win our class, but we even won the best general effect caption award.

The week between district and regional Mr. Haggard had the Marching Huskies compete at the Kokomo Invitational, hosted by our cross-town rivals, and the Norwell Invitational. Once again at Kokomo, we competed in exhibition at 10:45 A.M. because even though we weren't really the host we shared the same city.

After that performance we hopped on buses and traveled north to Norwell High School in the pouring down rain. No thanks to the rain, we performed in the gymnasium. On the other hand, our inside standstill proved to be to our advantage. The band won first place in Class B and the best music caption award beating East Noble, a tough competitor and a state finalist band, by one-tenth of a point. Mr. Haggard beamed from ear-to-ear, a proud moment for him and for us.

The night before our do-or-die regional contest our band boosters had a rally for us in the hopes of hyping our souls. We practiced for three hours, from 6 to 9 P.M. When we ventured inside to the band room, Mr. Haggard showed us the band's 1983 performances on the VCR. I'm not sure if it was the rally or what clicked my freshman-oriented brain that changed my opinion about marching band for the rest of my high school years and then some.

The ISSMA Regional contest became as important to us as the district contest that particular year. The entire Haworth High School student body found out the school board planned to consolidate the two city high schools into one for the next school year. The "new" high school would be named Kokomo, of course, leaving the Haworth students without anything of their own. The only item we kept was the C.V. Haworth Building where grades 10–12 would be. The eighth and ninth graders would be at the old KHS building downtown. Neither building was big enough to have freshmen with the upperclassmen. That didn't matter to me because I would remain in the same building.

As I was saying, the regional contest was very important to us. That year was the last possible year for us to go to state finals as a school. Since the contest was on our own football field, we couldn't very well practice on it so we rode those fancy yellow school buses to Western High School, a 15-minute drive west of Kokomo. We didn't practice very long, maybe an hour at most, but at least the show was fresh in our minds.

On October 15, 1983, at 3:43 P.M., after singing "You'll Never Walk Alone" huddled together in warm-ups as we always did, the Haworth Marching Huskies performed our show dedicated to two band members who were killed in a car accident on their way to school. After our shining performance, we stood at the fence while the awards were handed out.

At the regional contest the division trophies were handed out first then the top five state finalists were announced. Let me explain this better. Like district each band had to score a certain amount of points in order to earn a Division I trophy. The top five scoring bands earning this trophy were then eligible for state finals in Terre Haute.

We earned a Division I, which was good, but we didn't make state. We were seventh, two places away from going to state finals.

Concord, Eastbrook, Winchester, Maconaquah, and Lebanon were the north Class B bands who made state finals.

The walk from the football field to the band room seemed longer than ever that day. I fought back the tears because I hadn't cried after any contest all season. Why did I have to start then? I hadn't had a reason to cry until that particular moment. Outside the band room doors, other members wandered around aimlessly. The seniors were especially hit hard. I sat down on the curb in a daze not knowing what to say or do. Marching band meant more to me than what I realized. What would happen next year with the consolidation? Would the band be as good as this year? Kokomo's band didn't compete in ISSMA, and since their director would be the "new" one, would he even compete like we had this year? I decided I couldn't worry about that now.

Mom found me still sitting on the curb about halfway in tears. I hugged her hoping the hug would make me feel better, but that failed. I was miserable and didn't believe that feeling would ever go away. All of my feelings of disliking marching band disappeared, and I wished this season could have been rewound and done again. Mom tried to make me feel a little better. She had been a judge's assistant during the contest. She informed me that the judge had disliked our handmade uniforms; they were part of our problem. How could he judge us based on our uniforms? How dare he. I bet if we had marched in our birthday suits he wouldn't have scored us low.

Later, Mr. Haggard told us, "We came within three points of taking top honors." The Marching Huskies were so close yet so far away.

A week later the band received a chance to redeem ourselves by competing one more time in the Marching Bands of America Regional championships at Lawrence Central High School in Indianapolis. This contest was (and still is) a national one, one that involved bands from across the United States. We performed in the preliminaries at 10 A.M., and even though we didn't make it to the evening finals, the band outscored Eastbrook.

In the November 4, 1983, *Kokomo Tribune,* Western's band director commented that Haworth should have gone to state finals.

19

I'm not sure about the rest of the band, but I felt better about our season, especially with comment like that coming from a band that did make it state in a different class. Impressive to say the least.

The band performed at the new city building dedication, but my teeth were killing me so I didn't go. (I had just gotten braces put on, and four permanent teeth pulled to make room.) I also managed to be sick (I really was) for the Veteran's Day parade. You never really missed much marching in a parade like that because no one really watched this kind of a parade unless it is like the Indy 500 or the Kentucky Derby parades.

Once we got through the fall marching season, nothing much happened except the tension over the consolidation. Haworth and Kokomo students were upset because we went through changes. Nothing would be the same next year. These changes hurt me a little. I had only been at Haworth for one year and hadn't really gotten too attached. My biggest fear, as I have already mentioned, was what kind of an effect the consolidation would have on the marching band. The school board's decision made Kokomo somewhat famous because of the publicity it received from the three Indianapolis TV stations. In fact, I was even on the news. Well, actually as it hung on a chair, my wool, blue and gold senior jacket showed its back to the camera as well as my flesh and blood back. I was famous and didn't know it until the next day after the news aired.

My infatuation with Rick Springfield continued into my freshman year. During a varsity basketball game I played in the pep band (Band B to be exact. We were divided into two groups, and the two directors took turns.).

Mr. Murray asked one of the golddusters, the girls who danced at halftime, "What song are you going to do?"

I thought the girl said, "'Human Touch' by Rick Springfield," but I was unsure.

Mr. M turned around to face us and said, "'Human Touch' by Rick Springfield," and pointed at me.

My small button of Rick was on my shirt.

As the school year neared its end, the realization of Haworth High School's demise dampened students' spirits. The marching band did their best to remember the 16 years of the school's existence. The band boosters helped us celebrate and/or commemorate those years with a party on Monday, May 14, 1984, a date forever etched into my memory, not to mention it was exactly one week after my 15th birthday, not that you probably care about that. A fun-filled evening for the band's last stand happened in the high school cafeteria where we shared whatever memories we had. I didn't have much to share since I had only been a Marching Husky for a year, but I did still feel as though I had been an important part of the school's awesome, or at least, in my opinion it was, marching band program.

As part of our last stand, our farewell evening, each band member received several souvenirs: a key chain resembling a theater ticket; a blue, laminated placemat with a picture of a husky on the left and the words to the school song on the right; a 33-rpm record of one band recorded several years earlier; a plastic, dark yellow mug with the school's coat of arms and the year printed in dark blue; my chenille "H" that I shouldn't have earned until my senior year; and most importantly, a gold piece of paper with every band and staff members' John Hancock scribbled on it in black ink.

My last duty as a Haworth band member included playing for the last graduation ceremony for the Class of 1984. I was glad I was a part of the ceremony and felt as though I was a major part of the school's history then.

On the last day of school, I walked out of the building knowing I would return as a "Wildkat" in just a little over two months when the marching band began two weeks of band camp. In all honesty I really wasn't looking forward to becoming a member of a 250-member band, afraid we wouldn't be as good as we had been in the past.

Because of this consolidation, the Haworth band didn't go to Florida as planned. Instead, the money was used to buy new uniforms since neither school had enough for 250. I thought it might have been neat to let each school wear their old uniforms, but I never told anyone that for fear he/she would laugh loudly in my face. Besides, that wouldn't have helped with the unity of the two schools, and we needed all of the unity we could get especially since we were upset enough about the consolidation. Oh, well, I tried not to worry any more than absolutely necessary. I guess I would discover soon enough just what the 1984 marching season would be like.

♫

Chapter 3

The transition from being one in 100 to becoming one in 260 wasn't as difficult as I thought it would be. In fact, the transition was easier than I thought it would be. A group of parents from each school, including my own mom, came together and helped the band and staff deal with this unity issue. The staff was also a combination of directors from both schools. Norman Walker of Kokomo High School became the head director, and Denny Farmer also of KHS became of the assistant directors as well as color guard instructor during sixth period class and for marching band. They were at the KHS south campus or the C.V. Haworth Building, the building where Haworth High School had been, with grades 10–12. Mr. Haggard became the associate director (What a title!) with Mr. Murray's assistance. They ended up at the KHS downtown campus with the eighth and ninth graders.

At first, I wasn't sure I liked having two new directors. I had hoped that either Mr. Haggard or Mr. Murray would stay with the upperclassmen, but neither one did. I was stuck learning how these new directors would teach. My first impression of the directors wasn't all that great. In fact, I thought Mr. Walker was a grumpy old man. He was in his late 40s, just a few years older than my parents, stood a little taller than me, probably five foot nine inches with a slender build. He wore glasses and didn't really smile or laugh very often, but he could if he wanted to do so. Mr. Farmer was probably in his late 20s, stood six foot two inches, and had a loud voice you listened to when he spoke. He seemed like he belonged teaching young men how to march in the Marines or the Army rather than teaching high school band students how to march.

Our first official rehearsal for the 1984 marching season was Monday, August 6, from 5 to 9 P.M. We rehearsed like that for the whole week preparing us for two weeks of all-day band camp at the high school. I wasn't really looking forward to band camp because I was usually pretty tired by the end of it. However, the good thing about it was that we only had to suffer for two weeks and then the misery was over. This band camp's times were different than what we had done the year before. We started bright and early at 7:15 A.M. each day, which meant staying up into the wee hours of the morning were out of the question, and we got to go home at 5:30 P.M. to eat supper and go to bed early. In a way I liked band camp structured like this. I could be at home to relax and sleep instead of a hot dorm room and a hard mattress for a bed; I could sleep in my own bed and an air-conditioned house.

By the end of the second day, I was a little sunburned, which I didn't know was possible. I was dark-complexioned and rarely burned when out in the bright sunshine for a short or a long time. However, this particular band camp was proving me wrong because on the third day I really got sunburned, especially the back of my right leg. In fact, Mom believed it to be sun poisoning so she told me I should wear sweat pants or long pants to protect it from getting any worse. You can imagine how I felt having to wear dark blue sweatpants for the rest of band camp.

Considering we were 260 strong when we started, they sure dropped like flies by the time two weeks of band camp was over. We were down to around 215. I really didn't think band was all that tough, but apparently, the 45 who dropped out did. We didn't really want them in our organization anyway, especially if they were going to keep us from reaching our goals.

On Sunday, September 2, 1984, the "new" Kokomo Marching Wildkats had their first big performance, performing for the very first Indianapolis Colts' football game. The newbies marching for the newbies. My memories of that day aren't as good as I would have liked them. We were stuck in a huge room with two big screen TVs, one in each end. They did feed us lunch before our performance, which was amazing considering the way they treated us later on the field.

We had to stuff into the space between two huge doors, air locks they called them. They warned us to hang onto our hats when they opened a door behind us because the air blew very hard, hard enough that it could have blown off your hat. Inside the Hoosier Dome, as it was known back then, was unbelievable, the only word that came to mind at the moment. The top was like a hot air balloon, and people sat all around us, although they didn't pay much attention to us. They were there to see 22 grown men beat each other trying to get a little brown weird-shaped ball to the opposite end of the field and score. Despite that, we marched what time we could on the AstroTurf. You wanted to make sure you rolled your feet, or you would end up on your nose flat on the ground. We hardly marched onto the field when the officials started yelling at Mr. Walker to get us off the field. We only performed the opener that lasted around three or four minutes before we were hustled off the field. So much for our 15 minutes of fame.

Our first contest of the 1984 marching season was an early one for us on September 8. I was out of bed early that morning since we left for Jennings County High School at 6 A.M. with a performance time of 2:15 P.M. We did fairly well considering we marched and played the first two songs and then did a standstill for the last song because we hadn't learned the drill for that it yet. We placed third out of four bands in Class AAA, a class for the largest bands, and then fifth overall. I can't recall who the first two place bands were, but we did beat Avon, a band we would continue to compete against.

Mr. Walker practiced us hard the next week in the hopes of not only improving our scores but finishing our show. After marching in our street clothes at the varsity high school football game the night before because we didn't want to dirty our clean uniforms for some boring football game, we competed in the third annual Pride of Paoli

Invitational in southern Indiana on September 15, another long trip on those gross yellow school buses.

At this contest we performed in a preliminary contest to see if we would make the evening finals, much like the Bands of America contest we had done the previous year. I don't know about the rest of the band, but I was almost worn out before we ever got to the football field. We marched what seemed like miles up and down hills to the football field, which in fact sat on a hill. Paoli is located in the hills and hollers. If you think that was tough, I bet it was really bad for the dads who pushed equipment, drum major podium and pit instruments up and down those hills.

Mr. Walker was happy with our performance. We competed against not only Indiana bands but some Kentucky bands as well. We were first runner-up in our class and third overall out of 14 bands. We didn't get home until 2:30 A.M. I sure slept well that night.

The band continued practicing its four days a week getting ready for our most important contests coming up later. This week's practices prepared us for our own invitational, the Tournament of Champions, on September 22. Drum majors for that year included a member from each band, a senior from KHS and a junior from HHS. I think this was just one more way of uniting the two bands. The drum majors directed 222 band members, including 36 color guard and 26 in percussion, to the tunes of "Rhapsody in Blue," "Sud a la Cuidad Del Oro (South of the City of Gold)," and "All Night Long," a popular song at the time sung by Lionel Richie—one of my personal favorites.

As before, since we hosted the contest, we didn't get to compete as the other bands did for a sparkling gold trophy to take home. All we could do was work on improving our score for the ISSMA District contest the following week. The winners of the four classes this year, if you care to know, were Anderson Highland – Class A, Lawrence North – Class B and overall (second was Center Grove—remember these two bands, will you?), Lewis Cass – Class C, and Frankton – Class D. It sure didn't seem like the winner changed much, which I never thought seemed fair. Then again life isn't fair. In fact, A and B stayed the same, and the D winner moved up a class.

Even though our score improved at our invitational, Mr. Walker was still worried about whether we would make it from district to regional. We had to score at least 70 to advance to regional, and most of the Class A scores around the state were lower than that. However, Mr. Walker was relieved when he learned they lowered the 70 to a 60. Too many other bands weren't scoring high enough. If the ISSMA people hadn't lowered the scores, there probably wouldn't have been any bands at regional.

On September 29, at 3:30 P.M., at what I always considered the most important contest of the season, the newly consolidated Kokomo High School competed in the 1984 ISSMA District contest. Based on my individual performance, I thought I gave a great performance except for a minor goof, or perhaps major goof, depending upon where you stood. In the last song I had the important job of leading a line of other clarinets as well as flutes toward the back of the field. The goof happened when I lost count and turned around two counts too early. Luckily for me, the rest of the line kept right on moving past me. I had just hoped no one had seen me do it except for the gal right behind me. Martha laughed about it later.

Even with my minor, or major, goof, the band got a Division I and moved onto regional. Mr. Walker told us later that we had scored above a 70—a 70.9 to be exact. Whew! We would have barely made it under the old scoring system. He also told us we had placed second behind Lafayette Jefferson, usually a tough competitor and a state finalist. How strange. The ISSMA people lowered the required score, and we still achieved the 70 we needed.

The Saturday between district and regional we competed at the Marching Bands of America Regional in Joliet, Illinois, a suburb of Chicago. This long band trip was one I'm sure won't be easily forgotten. We left the high school at 6 A.M. for the long bus ride north. I don't remember much what happened until we had practice on a football field surrounded by a fence. The downer was when the rain began to pour. We got on the buses, drove close to where we would compete, and ate supper at a couple of fast food joints. We traveled into the stadium where the rain poured again as we were changing into uniforms; however, the rain forced a delay. We sat on the buses waiting to see what the officials were going to decide.

After an already long day, we were ready to get the competition over so we could go home. We did end up marching, and the new debate become whether we would wear our white plumes. Just minutes before we marched onto the field, the plumes went atop our blue and white hats. That was a huge mistake, a very huge mistake. We shouldn't have used the plumes because as we prepared to perform the rain began to lightly sprinkle. The more into the performance we progressed the harder it rained. By the time we finished, the rain was coming down pretty hard. Our pretty feathers atop our hats stunk like dead chickens. There's no other way to describe the nasty smell. Needless to say, about 25 of them were ruined, no thanks to a band mother, who shall remain nameless here, who wanted us to wear them.

By the time we changed out of our uniforms, the rain was just a mist. We received fifth place out of 12 bands. Although our score dropped four points, Mr. Walker seemed okay about our performance, especially since we were only one of two Indiana bands there. After awards we returned to Kokomo arriving back at the high school at 3 A.M.

We practiced hard the following week for our second most important contest of the season, ISSMA Regional. I didn't know about the rest of the band, but I thought we had done a pretty good job of putting together a show considering two-thirds of the band, the eighth and ninth graders, had never marched a step in their lives before. That was what made us so remarkable, not to mention that we had been two high schools the year before, big cross-town rivals, and now we were the newly united Kokomo High School preparing for our do or die situation.

On October 13 we headed to Marion (a town later made famous by actress Julia Roberts when she wed singer Lyle Lovett, but anyway back to what I was saying) for a 1:46 P.M. performance against 10 other bands. As before, we had to receive a Division I rating as well as a top five score in order to make state finals. Just like

28

the year before, we obtained our Division I trophy but fell short of the score; we finished seventh out of 11 bands which wasn't too shabby. I certainly wasn't as disappointed as I had been about that time the year before. In fact, I had this gut feeling that somehow we would do better next year. I don't know why I felt that way, but I just did. Oh, well, stay tuned for next year.

Normally, if we didn't make state finals, we would have been done with the marching season at this point. However, Mr. Walker had decided we would compete in a Marching Bands of America Grand Nationals at the Hoosier Dome in Indianapolis in November. Anyway, we ended up with almost a month's worth of rehearsals. That is, a month's worth of freezing our buns. I couldn't believe how cold it got a couple of days. It got so cold that I couldn't even move my fingers to play my clarinet.

This competition was somewhat similar to the Paoli contest we did earlier in the season. Forty-nine bands began competing late Friday afternoon, November 16, and continued until late Saturday afternoon, November 17. Once the bands, coming from all over the United States, including a total of 13 states, finished competing, the officials announced the Top 12 finalists, those who competed that evening.

Having competed at 2:15 P.M. on Saturday, we didn't have to wait long to discover we hadn't made the evening finals. I think we knew without a brain surgeon telling us that we wouldn't make finals. Who were we kidding? Especially with bands such as Lafayette Jefferson, Western, Fort Wayne Northrop, and Ben Davis, an ISSMA state finalist band from the south regional and the only band in the south who outscored us, competing. By the way all did make the MBA Finals. In other words, if Kokomo had been south, we would have made state finals. (Doesn't that stink?)

In appreciation for our hard work, about 100 band members stayed and watched the finals, which featured the best 12 high school bands I had ever seen. We received the chance to see the United States Air Force Drum and Bugle Corps from Colorado Springs, Colorado, as we waited on the judges to tabulate the scores. To say the drum and bugle corps was awesome is an understatement, but I don't know what other word I could use to describe them. None of the Indiana bands won, but Western was fifth. We cheered for them because our drum major's girlfriend played an instrument, trumpet if memory serves me right, in their band.

As I stated earlier, the season would have ended with regional. However, that year it kept spreading out over the calendar farther and farther. On Sunday, February 17, the band was invited to play for an Indiana Pacers' game. How exciting—except this was a year that the Pacers stunk. Unfortunately, because of bad weather, our performance at the game was postponed until Thursday, March 14. We didn't get to sit up in the bleachers, but instead we sat on folding chairs at one end of the floor. Being short I couldn't see much of the game, which wasn't very much fun for me. We didn't even win the game for Pete's sake. They lost 113–112 against the Los Angeles Clippers.

Our last and most important event of our 1984, actually now 1985, marching season was our performance and competition at the Kentucky Derby in Louisville. We practiced a couple of weeks before we left for the marching competition and parade.

At 2 P.M. on Wednesday, May 1, the Marching Wildkats left on our three- to four-hour journey to Louisville. We were late arriving for the competition, but luckily they let us perform after our trip down there. Where we performed, the Commonwealth Convention Center, was nowhere near a regular football stadium. The floor and walls were concrete, and the bleachers weren't very high as most usually were.

Well, we did better than expected. I really didn't think we would do that well because we had to rush around once we arrived, which usually kept your concentration level down and the stress levels elevated. We competed against two of tough Kentucky bands, one of whom had beaten us at Paoli. After our performance all of the bands lined up for a retreat on the field. We stood at parade rest, absolutely no moving, as the judges announced the caption award winners, none of which we won.

As the judges announced the top three winners, I held my breath. We were not third, not second, so I relaxed thinking there is no way we could have won because we had won no caption awards. Usually, a band doesn't win a contest without having won at least one caption award. However, the Kokomo Marching Wildkats became an exception. When the announcer said we had won, we stood frozen to the floor, not only because we weren't supposed to move but because we were in shock, or at least I was. I had to laugh, though, a freshman clarinet player who stood directly in front of me started jumping up and down and screaming until she looked around, realized no one else was, and she fell back into parade rest. You should have seen us once we could move—everybody hugging each other, screaming. We were so happy. Mom told me later that one of my classmates, a tall, skinny baritone player, was so happy that when he hugged her he had picked her up off the ground and Mr. Farmer had to rescue her.

We were still flying high when we arrived at our hotel for some hopeful sleep. I had a heck of a time getting relaxed so I could fall asleep because the phone kept ringing, and when I finally did get to sleep, the phone rang and woke me up. We were supposed to tour the Louisville Slugger Factory, but we didn't get to do that. (I can't remember why.) We did get to tour Churchill Downs where the fastest two minutes happens every year on the first Saturday in May. I thought that was exciting and interesting since I would probably never see it again or attend the race. Without the bat factory tour, we ended up with extra time before our shining, actually rainy, performance in the Pegasus Parade, televised nationally. We ended up at a mall where we shopped and ate some lunch. That mall was a pretty neat one, one I could go back to visit providing I could find it in downtown Louisville again.

For the parade, we were considered special since we were the grand champion. The parade officials had a trophy banner placed in front of us as we marched down the streets. Once our part of the parade was done at 4:30 P.M., we loaded and prepared for our trip back home.

Back in Kokomo, I was taking a one-semester journalism class, and on Fridays, the teacher always gave us a 10-point quiz plus one or two bonus questions about news that had happened during the week. Our bonus question this particular Friday was "How did the band finish?" Practically everyone in the room turned to the back and looked at me, dressed in my souvenir T-shirt and nylon blue band jacket, looking to see if I would give them some sort of hint as to how we had done. I just smiled and looked up at the teacher; she smiled back. As we graded the quizzes in class, the teacher asked me the answer to the bonus question. At that moment I couldn't have been prouder to be a Marching Wildkat but not for long.

Sometime between the Pacer game and the Kentucky Derby contest, Dad came home with the news that the electric company he worked for was doing away with his job, the job that had forced us to move to Kokomo. He was transferred to a small town 30–40 miles south of Indianapolis called Martinsville. Even though I was going to miss the directors and the band in Kokomo, I was looking forward to starting anew. My main reason for missing the band was one big reason, I figured after we had done so well at the Derby that this band could or would make state finals in the next few years without me. State finals were something I dreamed about doing, marching in the Dome with nine other top Class A bands. I wasn't looking forward to a new marching band, especially not knowing what they did as far as contests went. Did Martinsville compete in ISSMA? If they did, how good were they? Had they made state finals? Questions instantly popped up in my head.

As Kokomo prepared to do summer band right after school was out, I prepared to move over an hour away and leave them behind. However, I got a crazy notion in my head, and Mom asked Mr. Walker about it. Can you believe I wanted to march summer band and learn a whole new show, complete with music and drill? Can you believe how crazy I was? Mr. Walker never really gave Mom an answer, though, so all I could do was wait.

At our first combined band banquet, one of the former Haworth band moms wished me good luck with my new band in Martinsville in front of everyone. Wow! That made me feel like I was truly going to be missed. What an ego booster!

During the last week of school, Mr. Walker stopped me outside the band room and asked me, "Michele, would you like to march in summer band?"

Without much hesitation, I said, "Yes," although I don't know why.

How could I have been so crazy to want to learn a new show for just three contests in June? I wouldn't even get to see how much they perfected their show for the fall unless Martinsville wasn't competing or unless Kokomo just happened to make state finals and Martinsville didn't. However, this marching would keep me in practice for Martinsville and at the same time would also keep my mind off of what was happening at home.

♫

Chapter 4

On Saturday, June 1, the day after Mr. Walker asked me to march summer band, I started rehearsal with the band. After being told I would be an alternate, it took only one day for me to earn a permanent spot. I really had a lot of fun with this. Here I was finally an upperclassman with my coordination problem under control. Obviously, the problem that plagued me two years earlier must have disappeared; otherwise, I wouldn't have earned a permanent spot or even the privilege of marching at all. Thanks, Mr. Walker. Not only did I earn that spot, but Mr. Walker informed me about the adoption. What adoption? He informed me that I was going to live with him, that I wasn't moving one and a half hours away to Martinsville.

On the following Wednesday we started band camp. We learned 11 charts that first day, which was a record. Usually, you could only get through maybe half that amount. We continued learning charts over the next week or so. I had so much more fun, so much more fun that I wished the adoption that Mr. Walker had joked about would really happen. Why was I having fun? I felt important. Of the clarinets on my side of the field, I was in charge of placing three others in their correct spots. I hated to see the month of June end because I wouldn't have the choice then; I would be moving, no more placing the younger ones in their spots. In fact, I probably would be more like a freshman in Martinsville, having to learn that band's ways and being low on seniority even though I was a junior. The thought of that made me unhappy.

As part of summer band, we marched, or more like participated, in three contests, two the weekend of June 14–15 and one on June 22. The band ended up with three new drum majors for the new marching season. Of the previous drum majors, one graduated from high school, and the other one decided he wanted to march with the Star of Indiana Drum and Bugle Corps. I don't know why you would skip marching your senior year in high school to do something like that, but that was his decision. To me it would have been something you could have done once you graduated. Anyway, two seniors and one junior became the new drum majors. (Remember the student who picked up my mom after we won Derby? This junior was the guy.) They directed the coolest show, the best music I had ever played while a band member: "Finale to Seventh Symphony" by Mahler; "Fire Dance;" and "She Believes in Me" by Kenny Rogers. I thought the drill was awesome, too, and I was beginning to wish I was going to be around in the fall.

On Friday, June 14, we left at 1 P.M. for our first contest at Chesterton in northern Indiana. It felt strange for me leaving on a band trip without Mom. She was always there for every band trip; she had been the head chaperone person who worked closely with Mr. Walker to get the trips organized. She was getting everything coordinated for our big move—you know, selling one house, buying another, packing all of our many belongings, including that ever so growing Rick Springfield collection. How would I manage without her there? However, I did have another band mom, Mrs. Scholl, looking out for me, a mom whom my mom had become good friends.

Like my early years in band, I don't really remember very much about these contests, only the basic need to know kinds of details. After competing in the Chesterton contest, marching the show and doing a retreat, we spent Friday evening in a gym, but at the moment I can't recall where, just a high school. We were supposed to visit the Indiana Dunes the next morning, but the rain kept us from doing that so like in Louisville the directors decided to take us to a mall in Merrillville.

Our second contest that weekend was on Saturday evening at Herscher, Illinois. Mr. Walker had a practice on the itinerary, but we didn't get much of one after it rained. We were lucky we even got to compete. On the other hand, we might have wished we hadn't gotten to compete after we found out how we finished. I really don't know why we even bothered doing these contests when we barely knew the show, but I guess Mr. Walker knew best, just like Father, right? I suppose the results were a way for him to see how the band was doing and what needed to be done in order to improve our scores.

Mr. Walker told us at Monday's rehearsal we finished sixth out of six bands at Chesterton and fifth out of seven bands at Herscher. At least we improved in placings. I guess it wasn't too bad considering we were probably one of the few bands who actually learned a whole new show. The rest of the bands used the previous fall's show.

Our last competition of the summer was the Bands of America Summer Nationals at the University of Wisconsin, Whitewater. This competition was much like the one where we competed in the Hoosier Dome the proceeding fall. We left on charter buses for our trip at 1 P.M. on Friday, June 21. I couldn't really tell how long the drive took. We were on the buses for nine hours, three hours of which was spent driving just through Chicago in rush hour traffic on Friday evening. Remind me to avoid that the next time, will you?

We spent the night in a school gymnasium in Janesville. (What a coincidence! Dad's aunt and uncle used to live there.) We were up early the next morning to prepare for our 9 A.M. open class performance. We had a short drive to the university. As we warmed up, one of the guard instructors realized the guard's capes hadn't been loaded, and no spare time was available to return. Actually, now that I think about it, I think it was a band mom, but I could be wrong. That mistake cost us on our scoring because, if I remember right, the guard had to have something in their hands at all times. Without the capes, they had nothing for a portion of the show. Out of the 19 or 20 bands competing, we were second to last.

Since we didn't make the top 12, a busload, including me, stayed behind to watch the finals. I really liked watching these really good bands perform. It was amazing to me that they were just high school students, kids like me, and not professionals. They moved with such precision, and the music sounded professional. Incredible is the only word that comes to mind. As one last note about our BOA performance, we were the only band using a show designed for the next school year. However, that would be an advantage to the band in the fall. Why? It had already been critiqued three times, and Mr. Walker would know exactly what needed to be done in order to perfect the show.

During one of my family's last days in Kokomo, Mom and I ventured to the high school in the hopes Mr. Walker would be there. We wanted to tell him we were leaving town and say a final good-bye. I couldn't believe I was being forced to move once again, now especially when I had something I enjoyed in my favor, a band and staff who were working hard to achieve the same goal, state finals.

Even though I said earlier it would be a chance of renewal for me, I didn't realize how much my leaving meant to the band until a couple of weeks later when I got the mail out of our yucky brown barn-like mailbox in Martinsville. My name and address appeared on a business envelope but there was no return address. I didn't get excited because I figured it was either junk mail or a chain letter. I almost didn't even open it. However, once I was in the house, my curiosity got the best of me, and I decided to open the envelope. Inside was a short note from Mr. Walker telling me how much he appreciated me in his band and how he knew I would be an asset to my new band. The following is the note in his exact words:

Dear Michele,

I am writing to tell you how much we appreciated your special dedication and hard work while in our band. Your work attitudes and high moral character speaks very well of you and your family.

You must understand that the next few months will be tough being the new kid in the band, but keep that chin up and be yourself, and it won't be long and those around you will recognize that you are a special person who will be important to their program.

Best of luck to you, and again thanks for that special dedication.

Respectfully,
Norman Walker

That note touched me deeply, and I knew from then on I would be just fine.

♫

Chapter 5

About a week before my first band practice with Martinsville, Mom and I went to the high school to sign up for classes, see if we could meet the band director and obtain a practice schedule. Having no idea what he looked like, Mom and I hung around where the music department—or rather, I would learn, the music suite. I was surprised when the director turned out to be much younger than Mr. Walker. In fact, I believe my new band director could have been his son. Anyway, Mom did most of the talking; she was good about getting all of the details or most important information that we needed to know.

As Mom talked to this tall stranger, all I could do was think this man, his name being James Brenneman, was going to be my band director for the next and last two years of my high school career. He was tall, as I've already mentioned, much taller than Mr. Walker, probably over six foot would be my estimate; he was in his late 20s and married, or at least a gold band on the third finger of his left hand told me he was. All I hoped for was that he was a good director who pushed us to achieve whatever goal we set.

On Monday, July 15, from 6 to 8:30 P.M., I attended my very first practice as a Martinsville Marching Artesian or an Artesian Showband member. I preferred the first name as opposed to the last because it sounded so much more 1980s. Artesian Showband? What kind of a name was that anyway? The second name was an older name the band was trying to get away from being called.

Anyway, Mr. Brenneman started rehearsal by giving a little spiel about what would happen during the 1985 marching season, introduced the staff, and passed out music. Within a half hour he finished talking, and we worked outside on fundamentals as he called them. Mr. Walker always called them basics so already I was dealing with something new. Mr. Brenneman paired me up with a girl who was my age and my squad leader. She helped me with whatever I didn't know how to do and helped me learn the ropes.

Do you remember how worried I was that this band didn't do the ISSMA contests like Kokomo? Well, I no longer had a need to worry because not only did we do ISSMA, but we also did a competition at the Indiana State Fair, a contest similar to BOA except the bands were not as good. Wow. We had to learn a separate show just for the Band Day contest at the fair in August as well as a field show used for the September/October contests.

We practiced five nights a week for four weeks before we started a week of band camp during August 12–17. Gees, it seemed like a lot of rehearsing. In my opinion, I'm really not sure if I liked the way band camp was done. We didn't begin our mornings until 8:30 A.M. with an hour break at 11:30 A.M. for lunch. If it was unbearable outside, either heat or rain, we would practice music and maybe movements in the auditorium in small groups and then as a whole band inside until 3 P.M. Then we went back outside for an hour before having a two-hour supper break and returned at 6 P.M. for another two and a half hours of rehearsal. I was always glad when 8:30 P.M. rolled around because I was tired especially by the time Friday arrived.

I never thought I would have to worry about being initiated as a junior, but as a new member in the band, I had no choice in the matter. Luckily, the seniors were nice to me; I mean really nice. Most of the freshmen and other new members had shorts on, but I had worn jeans because of the cool evening, which I truly believe kept the seniors from doing much to me. Of course, they didn't get too awfully violent or abusive anyway.

On Friday night of band camp week, we performed our state fair show on the parking lot for the parents. This was a good thing to do because at least we had an audience before our first performance of the year—although they were a biased audience who would still love us no matter how bad we were.

After the performance we had a dance and an overnighter at the high school. The dance was in the cafeteria at the opposite end of the building, and the overnighter was in the music suite, the area where anyone who had anything to do with the music of our school hung out. Of course, the directors and/or chaperones separated the boys and girls. They sure knew how to ruin our fun.

We had one more dress rehearsal when we performed our show at the Red and Blue game before our big debut at Band Day. This game was an intra-squad game between the offense and the defense.

On Tuesday, August 20, after a five-year absence, the Martinsville Marching Artesians performed at the Indiana State Fair Band Day in the ninth spot. This was such a long day for all of us. After eating a hot meal at Ponderosa and going to a church on 38th Street for a rest break between the morning and evening competition, we returned to the fairgrounds for the evening competition. After making it into the Sweet 16, we placed ninth. We were really, really happy to say the least. Not too bad considering the band hadn't performed in the contest in five years. The bands we beat were probably trying to figure out where in the world we had come from. Maybe out of the blue?

Even though I missed Kokomo, I did still have some contact with the band director. Two days after Band Day on our way to our lake cottage, my family and I stopped in Kokomo and visited Mr. Walker.

A couple of weeks later on September 4, Mom returned to Kokomo to pick up my yearbook. After learning that they couldn't disturb the teacher to get the yearbook, Mom and Mrs. Scholl, my other "mom," went to the band room. Mr. Walker was outside with the band, but Mr. Farmer and the guard were in the hallway. They were getting ready to have practice.

Mr. Farmer said in his military voice, "Why don't you keep these girls quiet?" and turned around and walked away.

Mrs. Scholl said, "Do you know who you're talking to?"

He stopped, turned back around and looked at Mom; then he said, "Oh," and hugged her.

I wanted to see Kokomo compete at Paoli on September 14, but Mr. Brenneman decided to schedule a practice. Then he changed our contest on September 28 so that I couldn't go see Kokomo at their invitational. I figured since I had learned that show I might as well see it performed a few times, but I guess it wasn't supposed to happen. Gee, thanks, Mr. Brenneman, you sure have a way of spoiling a girl's fun. Mom got a letter from the Scholls. The Kokomo band was first runner-up at the contest they had gone to over the weekend and won caption awards for best percussion, which didn't surprise me because Mr. Murray was awesome, and the best field commander.

On Friday, September 20, we had our last performance before our first contest and appropriately enough in the Hoosier Dome for a football game. No one but me had ever marched in the Dome before, and I must say how I was very excited to be there again. The Dome is an overwhelming place, but it is also good practice since we would hopefully make state finals. Can you tell I am very determined to see a band I know and love go to state finals? I also love marching in the Dome. There is just something about being in such a huge place and performing on the AstroTurf. Maybe it's how high up the press box is; in order to get your instrument in the right place, you really have to get your chin up. Such a proud moment.

Well, maybe I was being a bit too optimistic when I said we would make state finals. I don't think I was thinking clearly. Saturday, September 28, proved we probably wouldn't be seeing the Dome again any time soon. We competed at two contests that day, Center Grove and Greenwood.

During the day at Center Grove High School, we placed sixth out of eight bands. We played "El Granito," "Blues in Hoss Flat," and "*Cats* Medley." Our senior and our junior drum majors led all 160 of us onto the field. Our staff besides Mr. Brenneman included George York, Eric Harris, and a few others.

Later that day at Greenwood High School, we faced the good, the bad and the ugly. We improved our score from the earlier contest by 10 points; we placed 10th; and only 10 bands competed. We were dead last. How terrible.

During the week's practices, the band worked hard because we wanted a first division at the ISSMA District contest. The following Saturday we headed for Southport High School on the south side of Indianapolis. We performed our cleaned-as-you-are-going-to-get-it eight minute show at 3:04 P.M. and earned ourselves a big Division I trophy. The band was happy because they hadn't been doing very well in the past few years.

What I had been used to at Kokomo, always getting Division I trophies, didn't always happen with Martinsville. In fact, either my freshman or sophomore year, they hadn't even made it out of district meaning they had received a Division II trophy. I couldn't imagine what that must have felt like. I always felt sorry for those bands, but I really did then, especially knowing I could have been in this band had my family moved sooner.

One thing my family learned when we moved to Martinsville was that the town is known for its Fall Foliage Festival, a festival that brings people from all over the state and sometimes even out of state. Naturally, the band had to march in the parade, supposedly the second biggest parade in Indiana after the Indy 500 parade, since we were the hometown school. Sunday, October 13, turned out to be like one of those hot, stinking summer days and being dressed in a wool uniform didn't make matters any better. My petite body for some reason or another didn't take too kindly to the heat.

During the pre-parade we had marched from the high school around to one of the elementary schools, probably a quarter to half mile. This is hard to describe, but the high school, one of the two middle schools, and one of the elementary schools are very close to one another. As we stood waiting for the parade to begin, I began to feel light-headed and dizzy. The longer I stood there the worse I felt; I knew I wouldn't make it through the two-mile long parade. Since I was almost in the last rank, I stepped out of line and started walking to the front part of the band hoping to find Mr. Brenneman.

When I found him, I said, "I'm not feeling very well. I think I'm going to pass out."

"You can go back to the high school," he said.

43

I had to walk clear across a big open field between the high school and the other two schools I mentioned earlier. By the time I arrived back at school, I felt even worse so I knew I had made the right decision.

The next day at school both Mr. Brenneman and sophomore Kay, one of my fellow clarinet players, asked me if I was feeling better.

I told them both, "Yes."

Kay had actually been standing next to me in the parade line-up.

That week at practice we concentrated on cleaning the drill as much as we could since ISSMA Regional would be on Saturday. We managed to get a lot done on the closer, or last song of the show, since it was the worst of the three songs we played. Little did I know that after I worked hard that week I wouldn't even get to march at the contest. I woke up on Friday morning with my bedroom spinning at full force; this might have also explained the way I had felt the previous Sunday for the parade. In fact, I felt as though someone had taken the foot of my bed and was trying to dump me off the head. I was so dizzy I could barely even stand up. My stomach was upset, and I was doing something too gross to even mention here. I was hoping it was just a 24-hour bug because I really wanted to march on Saturday. I had never missed a contest and wasn't about to start then.

When I woke up Saturday morning, October 19, I was still dizzy and weak from a lack of food. I knew then I would never make it through the day and would miss the most important contest of the season. Even though I didn't go, Mom and Dad still chaperoned and reported the results when they got home.

Without yours truly, the band ended up marching on the parking lot at Columbus East High School because of the rain. They didn't do very well at all, earning a Division II and ninth out of 16 bands. We sure seemed to be stuck on that ninth place thing. Mom called Mrs. Scholl later that evening. Do you remember how I learned a whole new show at Kokomo earlier in the summer? Well, they won the right to march that show at state finals in the Hoosier Dome. Can you believe that? I told you someone would make it. Sometimes I feel like I have a sixth sense about things, and this is one of those times when

I had that feeling. I made up my mind right then that I would go to state finals to watch them.

Six days after our fiasco at Columbus, the band followed the football team to Terre Haute North to pep them up for the first sectional game. After our halftime performance, North's band wished us good luck the following day at finals. Apparently, they were confused and mixed us up with another band that made it to state finals. I only wished it was us going.

Things really do happen I guess. I mean this in a sarcastic way. Due to unforeseen circumstances beyond my control, like my grandparents who decide to spend the day with us because they were leaving for Florida, I didn't get to see the Marching Wildkats march state finals in the Hoosier Dome. I wasn't happy to say the least. I had marched that show and wanted to see it in the Dome.

The Martinsville Band did the end of the marching season a little differently than Kokomo. First of all, they did it in October, not in May. They did a stadium review, including both middle schools, at the MHS gym. It really wasn't all that exciting, just parents and supporters in the audience. All of the bands performed the songs they had used during the marching season.

Our year ended the following evening with the annual band banquet, which was actually pretty nice even though I didn't win any awards. Overall, even though I lost out on marching with a state finalist band, my junior year as a Marching Artesian wasn't as bad as I thought it would be. In fact, it went a little beyond my expectations because we did everything about like I was used to doing at Kokomo, especially ISSMA, which was the best part about marching band, being able to compete with the other bands. I really don't see why some bands even exist without competing. Of course, if they don't know how it is in the first place, I guess it doesn't matter, does it?

♫

Chapter 6

I had heard many times that your senior year in high school was always the best, and I must say it rang true for me. Why was it the best? Not only was I on the newspaper and yearbook staffs, but I was also a squad leader for one of the best marching bands around. As a squad leader, I taught three others, usually all freshmen, how to march, just as I had done right after my sophomore year at Kokomo.

Mr. Brenneman decided to change summer band practices; the seniors, or maybe I should say squad leaders because not all were seniors yet, had to go in a day early as did the freshmen and any new members so they got an idea as to what marching band was all about. I had a blast with that because I was finally the one who got to do the yelling instead of the other way around. Revenge is sweet, isn't it? Anyway, being a senior in band made me feel important like all of my hard work was *finally* paying off.

Of course, being a senior could also have its down time like being assigned, along with one of my squad members, to march in a trumpet line for the entire field show. I didn't think my skinny black oversized recorder looked anything like the brassy horn the rest of them carried. Boy, was I fuming at home that night after practice! I told Mom and Dad what had happened.

All Mom could say was, "I'm sure he has a reason for doing that."

I kept thinking that maybe it was only a temporary situation, which my other squad member and I would meet with the woodwinds at some point in the show and would stay with them. However, that didn't seem to happen. We were always at opposite ends of the field.

Band camp was a hot, nasty week in which my nose turned a deep red the first day. This year instead of doing just an informal initiation the seniors, with a little prodding from Mr. Brenneman, decided to do a formal initiation, too. So, during band camp, we did the informal initiation on Thursday sparing the freshmen and new members from as much embarrassment as possible.

By the end of band camp week, I finally discovered why Mr. B, as we had started calling him now, had put me in the trumpets; on Friday as we learned the final moves of our show, my last spot was on the sideline somewhere between the 30 and 40 yard lines. (I can't recall right now exactly where.) I felt as though no one else was on the field but me because I couldn't see anyone else. Everyone in my line was behind me at a slight diagonal. I may be grasping for straws, but Mr. B knew this was a leader spot, a spot for someone like me. I even moved the whole line off the field as did two others. That made me feel even more important. While this feeling of importance roamed through my head, I decided that Mr. B wasn't such a bad guy after all.

On Friday evening of band camp week, we performed our state fair show twice for the parents and other supporters. The seniors then did the formal initiation. On the auditorium stage, candles were lit and placed between the trophies the band had won over the last few years. The freshmen, who were blindfolded once again, were led into the auditorium where they sat in the front rows; the rest of the band sat in the back. Any senior who wanted to say anything did. I wanted to say something, but I didn't have the courage to speak up in front of the others; I was a little shy. Okay, I'll admit it; I was really shy. I knew deep down that with a little encouragement this band could accomplish anything we put our minds to doing.

After the seniors who wanted to speak finished, one of the underclassmen said, "Let's hear it for the class of '87!"

Mr. B informed us seniors that we had done a nice job. Some of the seniors even hugged him; he patted me on the back, another sign that he didn't stick me in the trumpets on purpose.

On Tuesday, August 19, the 1986 Indiana State Fair Band Day gave us the chance to perform in front of a real crowd, not that our parents and huge band supporters weren't a real crowd, for the first time that year. We didn't do very well in the morning after performing in the 11th position. However, we did make it to the Sweet 16, or the night show, much to Mr. B's surprise.

We did improve our performance in the evening show, but we still placed ninth, the same place we received the previous year. The only good thing that came out of this was that we beat two bands, Edgewood and Alexandria, who had beaten us last year. I watched Band Day on TV the following Saturday night. It was strange watching our own band on TV.

Once school started, band practices really stunk. I don't think anybody really cared, so much for what the seniors said at formal initiation.

I even heard another staff member make the comment to Mr. B through the walkie talkies that "this was not the same band that had gone to fair."

Maybe I was wrong about my own opinion of the band; maybe we weren't as good as I thought we were. At the same time this was happening, Mrs. Scholl sent Mom a letter telling us that Mr. Walker was no longer the band director. He was hired as assistant principal at Lafayette Park Middle School, a middle school in Kokomo. She also told us that Kokomo would be at the Indiana State University and Greenwood invitationals. I only hoped we beat them.

The Friday before our first contest, the band performed at the Hoosier Dome during halftime for the football team. The surprise and reason I am even making a comment about this is because the Martinsville crowd actually clapped for us. Whether they did it out of pity for us or whether they liked our show, I don't know. At least they acknowledged us in some form or another unlike the usual when they ignored us.

On Saturday, September 20, we competed in our first two field show competitions of the season. At the Mid-States Marching Band competition at Indiana State University at Terre Haute, we performed at 5:37 P.M. Our senior and our junior drum majors led the band onto the field. Our repertoire included "Slaughter on Tenth

Avenue," "Tiger of San Pedro," and "Candle on the Water," the last song being the title song from *Pete's Dragon*. Besides Mr. B, Mr. Harris and several others taught us the fundamentals and drill.

The buses left for our first destination at 2 P.M. Beth, our senior drum major, and I walked to the restroom as soon as we got there. Now I don't normally tell anyone about me going to the restroom, but there is a funny story involved here so keep reading. I saw Mrs. Scholl standing in a concession stand line with other Kokomo band parents. I poked her on the shoulder and surprised her. I journeyed into the restroom and then waited on Beth.

A Kokomo band parent with a daughter one or two years younger than me came out of a stall, smiled at me in my MHS band uniform, washed her hands, smiled at me again, and started walking out the door.

She quickly turned around, grabbed my skinny arm, and said, "I know who you are!"

I thought I was going to split a gut laughing so hard.

After our hot, grueling performance and a group picture, I felt like I was overheated in the heavy wool uniform. I grabbed a cup of water, one of many being passed out, and headed for Mom.

She asked me, "Are you okay?"

Apparently, I even looked terrible. "I think I'm going to pass out," I said.

Mr. B saw me, put a hand on my shoulder, and asked if I was all right. He took my plastic white cowboy-looking hat off, put it on his head, and informed me I had a small head. No, Mr. B, your head is big. Within a few minutes I got on the bus for our next destination.

At Plainfield's Eighth Annual Marching Band Festival, we performed at 9 P.M. This must have been our fifth place day because we got fifth at both contests. Kokomo had luck on its side when they placed fourth at ISU. Well, we would just have to see what would happen next time if we competed against each other again.

I told you earlier that my senior year was probably the most memorable year for me, and here was another reason why. As part of homecoming week following our first weekend of contests, I was selected to ride in the back of one of two trucks in the homecoming parade. That was tons of fun riding down the streets of Martinsville trying to play an instrument while standing up in the back of a pickup truck. Imagine the coordination it took to do that. And I thought it was bad trying to stay on the correct foot my freshman year. Not to mention the joy of actually having people look at the band outside of Band Day. That was one thing that really disappointed me about this town. Once the band had competed at Band Day, the support for the ISSMA contests disappeared. Yeah, sure, the band won monetary awards at Band Day *if* they placed high enough, but the ISSMA contests got us so much more recognition. Band Day, what's that? ISSMA, oh, so your band made it to state finals. That's cool, really cool. See what I mean?

On Saturday, September 27, after only marching our opener during Friday night's football game because the field was really muddy, the band competed at Center Grove's Second Annual Cavalcade of Champions. Because of their muddy field, we competed on the parking lot with the audience sitting around the perimeter. Can you believe we got second place behind Greenwood? We also earned best drum major. Wow is all I can say. Someone must have been watching out for us, at least, at this contest, because we didn't fare very well at the evening one.

At the Greenwood Invitational we only marched onto the muddy field where we stood and played while the color guard did their routine in place. We received a participation plaque. The weirdest thing, or perhaps silliest was a better word, happened at this contest. Center Grove won the caption for best marching. How in the world could that happen when we didn't even march the shows? We also did one other good thing at Greenwood; we beat Kokomo by five points. I beamed at that one. Now we were even.

On the Thursday before our ISSMA District contest, the band went over our field show about 10 times I think. We were really hyped up. Think about it, though. We did pretty well last week, and we were feeling good about our show. In addition to our good feelings, this band had a great group of leaders, a little biased if you ask me, but who's asking?

On Friday, October 3, I sat in my sixth period publications class (I was on both the newspaper and yearbook staffs, remember?) when an announcement was made that the ISSMA District contest was postponed one week because of all the rain we had gotten. Instantly, I was upset, maybe even angry is a better word; I was ready for the contest on Saturday, not in a week. Our hype would disappear, and then we wouldn't do as well.

Later that evening as the band sat in the band room preparing to leave for the Dome game, Mr. B talked about an ISSMA article in the *Artesian Herald*, the one I had written for the school newspaper.

He told us, "I read an article in the *Herald*, and apparently, someone in this band thinks that we have the potential to go to state," and he looked to his left where I sat among the other clarinetists and smiled at me.

The week before district was not a good one for practices. We had our first really cold practice on Tuesday. Apparently, not many of us dressed for the cold weather so they were the ones freezing to death. I dressed as warmly as I could, and I was still cold. Anyway, because we were doing so terribly, Mr. B did a good job of getting mad at us, you know, yelling a whole lot. Who could blame him? District was on Saturday, and we acted like it was no big deal.

Thursday's practice was a little better but not by much. We marched downtown from West Middle School, played for Customer Appreciation Night of the Fall Foliage Festival, and wasted valuable practice time, but I guess we at least owed the town that much.

Our last home game and our last chance to play in front of a crowd happened on Friday night. The Class of 1987, the senior class might I add, was honored during halftime with the girls, including me, receiving a carnation and the boys a pin.

On Saturday, October 11, the band finally competed in the ISSMA District contest at Southport High School. We marched onto the field at 2:51 P.M. and, in my opinion, performed the show better than we had practiced it all week. I knew that was what we would do because it seemed like it happened in every contest we competed. We could have the worst practices in the world, but then when it came to the real thing, something clicked in all of our thick-skulled minds. I was afraid after we were hyped up for last week that we would let down this week. I must have been wrong on that one because we received a Division I and a score of 66 points. Mom chaperoned this trip.

After we found out we made regional, Mr. B asked her, "Will Michele be marching at regional this year?"

Remember how I was sick the year before and wasn't able to go? Mr. B was trying to joke around with Mom. Funny, Mr. B. See how hard I'm laughing?

I got lucky again that year for the Fall Foliage Festival parade. We lined up at the high school just like we did last year. However, as we walked the street to the actual starting point of the parade, it began drizzling rain and got a little harder to the point it was raining pretty good. Mr. B decided at that point we weren't going to march. He didn't want instruments wet not to mention the uniforms ruined for regional.

Before our last band practice and two days before the regional contest, Mr. B met with the seniors. He informed us that there were four bands, including us, fighting for the fifth spot for state finals. He was already guessing who the other four spots would be because they were always the same bands, you know Ben Davis, Center Grove, those bands that I have mentioned a million times already. Anyway, Mr. B seemed to believe we could make it if we really tried. Now what did I say earlier? Did I really have him believing I was right about us having the potential to make state finals? I do believe so.

On Friday night our one drum major decided to have a party for band members only, no staff. We watched the state fair and district contests on videotape. Many band members complimented me on my editorial. I was very pleased with myself since several of them liked it. I may not be able to express myself verbally, but I sure know how to write what I think.

Saturday, October 18, is a day the Marching Artesians won't forget, our most important contest of the season, ISSMA Regional at Bedford North Lawrence High School. We performed at 3:43 P.M.

I could tell by the way I felt and the way the crowd reacted at the end of our show that we had done a terrific job. I can't even begin to describe the feeling, but you can just tell when the band had done a kick butt kind of performance.

Now that I think about it a little longer, I got this tinkling feeling throughout my whole short body, perhaps adrenalin, made me want to put my chin even higher into the air and shout to the world, "Look at us. We've just performed the show of our lives."

As I led my long line off the grassy field and back to the buses, I just about couldn't stop feeling so proud. Even if we didn't make state finals, we still performed the best show of the year, and I was proud to be a Marching Artesian.

When award time came around, my good feeling was right. We received a Division I rating but didn't get the chance to go to state, didn't even come close, 10th out of 15 bands, scoring 70 points. What were the judges looking at?

At some point during our time at Bedford, Mrs. B told Mom, "I liked Michele's editorial," and apparently, Mr. B did, too.

Back at the high school band room, Mr. B had the whole band meet there. He said, "You underclassmen need to thank these seniors for a job well done."

All of the underclassmen clapped while tears swelled up in my big brown eyes.

Mr. B looked around the huge room at all of us seniors. He looked at me and smiled like he understood. In my very strong opinion, I think he was going to miss this senior class very much, but I could have been wrong.

After voting the previous week for whom we thought deserved the awards at the band banquet, the actual event happened on Tuesday, October 28. I gave Mr. B a letter telling him how much I enjoyed being in the Marching Artesians, a picture of him at the Plainfield contest (He stood like he was thinking about us really hard, like the *Thinker*. Dad had taken the picture. It ended up in the yearbook.), and a senior picture of me. I saw Mrs. B showing Mrs. Harris the picture I had given Mr. B.

As part of the awards, the seniors gave each of the staff members a T-shirt with some kind of saying printed on the front. Senior Sara Richmond handed them out. When Mr. B received his T-shirt that said, "March in the direction you're going," he hugged Sara. Mr. H's shirt said, "Good luck." I won't go into detail here, but there is a long story behind that one. In fact, I think I will spare him any embarrassment and not say anything else. He was already embarrassed enough when Sara gave him the shirt. His entire face turned beat red. The shirts were a way for each director or staff member to remember something they said repeatedly during rehearsals.

Beth won the Gary Hacker Memorial Award, an award in the memory of a student who had died, and received a hug from Mr. B. Roger, another fellow senior, cried when he received the award for Most Outstanding Bandsman. The seniors got wooden paddles with MHS Band engraved on one side and our names on the other. The previous year the whole band had signed them before they were given to the seniors; however, that year they ran out of time. We signed each other's paddles after the banquet. Mr. B signed mine. As he handed it back to me, he winked and smiled at me.

On Halloween night our football team played at Bloomington High School North. Much of the band was gone since it was fall break, and those who were there wore costumes as Mr. B told us we could if we chose. The highlight was after senior Brian played his tenor saxophone solo; he flashed the crowd with the trench coat he wore. (He had shorts and a T-shirt on underneath.)

On the following Monday Mr. B gave us his exciting news during band class. During the four-day weekend, Mrs. B went to the doctor and found out she was expecting. Everybody sure seemed happy for him. How exciting!

In my senior memory book, I had written about a few marching band memories. For my most memorable moment, I wrote, "When the band got a first division at the ISSMA Regional marching band contest," and under my happiest, "Mr. James Brenneman told us band kids that Mrs. Tracey Brenneman was going to have a baby." I also described Mr. B as my favorite teacher. He was the best because "he became a second dad to us band kids." Heck, we spent more time with him than we did with our real fathers in the summer and fall. On the good time and friends page one part was the best time we had as seniors, and I wrote, "was being in marching band. We worked our tails off to do well in the ISSMA contests and still had fun. I will never forget my senior year."

How true that was. By the time I graduated I was really wishing I wasn't. I just had the funny feeling the band was going to be even more deserving of the awards it would receive next year. You know most of the time I get a funny feeling about something I'm usually right. Well, I guess we'll see, won't we?

♫

Chapter 7

About a month after I graduated good things were already happening to Mr. B. He and Mrs. B became the proud parents of a boy on June 30. The band seemed to be working, too. I was constantly going over to the high school to watch rehearsals. Heck, I could barely hear them at our brown cedar-sided house just at the edge of town.

On Friday, August 21, as we had done every year at the end of band camp, the band performed their show in new uniforms, black or white pants and royal blue jacket. We always had two sets of pants. The black was usually for the morning show or football games and then white pants for the evening show and the ISSMA contests.

I should have been marching as a "super senior," but I had changed my mind at the last minute. According to Band Day guidelines, a band student who had just graduated in the spring could march in the show, hence, the name "super senior." As I watched them, I wished I hadn't been so much like a woman and hadn't changed my mind. Darn me. I had been measured for a new uniform when Mr. B had ordered them and had even told him I would march as a super senior. Then I had changed my mind, just like a woman.

They did their state fair show twice. On the second time through, the Marching Arties looked and sounded so good. These silly chills screamed up and down my back; the funny feeling gave me a sign.

On the following Monday, I picked up my pictures from wherever I had had them developed. (I can't recall now.) Of the five pictures I had taken, I placed one inside a precious greeting card wishing the band good luck.

When I arrived at the high school, I walked inside. It felt funny being there and not being in class as they were.

As I was going into the music suite, one of the junior band members hollered, "Michele."

Mr. B wasn't in his office, and knowing he was probably still in class, I waited around for a few minutes. I killed the minutes by looking at the bulletin board and by listening, or perhaps feeling, my heart beat. I admit I was a little nervous doing this. Other than to give a paper or answer any of his questions, I had never really carried on a conversation with Mr. B.

A few minutes later Mr. B, wearing a yellow polo shirt and pale blue pants, and some of the current band members came around the corner from the band room.

Mr. B chatted with them until he saw me and said, "Hey, guys, look who's come to visit us." I walked over to him and gave him the envelope.

He asked, "Can I read it now?"

I answered him with a, "Yes."

He read the card and said, "Oh, a picture." Both the card and the picture were tacked to the bulletin board where I had just studied everything that was on it.

Mr. B looked at me and asked, "Is that okay?"

I said, "Yeah."

The students had all left except for senior Ralph.

Mr. B asked me, "Why can't you go tomorrow?"

"I don't have a ride," I replied. (In the letter, I told him I couldn't go tomorrow.) The band had practice and ran through the show 10 million times or so it felt like. I just hoped they would do okay tomorrow.

I am glad, I mean really glad, I didn't go to Band Day because it was rainy and cold. Gosh, I can't imagine how miserable the kids were. Kids? I guess now that I was out of high school I didn't consider myself a kid anymore. How would you like to be stuck in a huge grassy field inside a dirt track with no shelter except those dreaded yellow buses? I also wouldn't want to march in that kind of weather either. My right knee always gave me fits when it was cold or even cool.

Instead, I listened to the contest on WCBK, the local radio station. The Marching Arties placed seventh, not too shabby if you ask me. I was so happy for them, happy that they finally broke the ninth place record. It was about time; two years in a row of being in ninth place was enough. I knew they would get into the Top 10.

A few days later highlights from the Sweet 16 were shown on an Indianapolis TV station. Junior Paul played his trumpet solo. They looked so good, and you know what they say about TV. That sometimes TV distorts the way things really are. I remember many times reading articles about a particular actor or actress saying they couldn't watch themselves on TV because they didn't like to see themselves like that. Watching them made me wish I had actually been there even more.

When I left for my first year at Indiana University, I continued following the band, not physically but mentally. Constant thoughts swirled around in my mind. I had no idea how much I was going to miss being in band until it was no longer there. I had thought about marching in the IU Marching 100, but they didn't compete. Why would I want to waste my time learning a different show for each home football game? If I couldn't compete, then I didn't want to do marching band.

I did sign up for the All-Campus Band, which met on Monday evenings and really wished I hadn't done that. It was so boring, and the bus situation was ridiculous, so ridiculous that I don't even want to discuss it here. Let's just put it this way. I didn't participate with this band ever again. Marching band was always my thing, not the symphonic or concert band.

On the Friday before ISSMA District, I stopped to visit Mr. B after school. He complimented me on my letter that appeared in the previous evening's newspaper.

"What time does the band perform tomorrow?" I asked him.

"How are you getting along with school?" he asked me.
I told him fine.

I went to the last home football game, which also happened to be senior night. No one was there, and I nearly froze to death, perfect weather for those running around in uniforms. How could I have been so silly to go and sit through a football game? Of course, the halftime entertainment was always good.

The band's big day was Saturday, October 3. Mom, Grandma Mathews, and Denise and Bruce Jones all piled, or maybe the word should be stuffed, into our maroon four-door Chevette. I never really realized how small that car is until you try to put five people into it to head toward ISSMA District at Southport. Denise was junior Lynn Jones's mom, and Bruce was Lynn's younger brother.

At 4 P.M. I was in total awe as I watched the band perform, such perfect intervals and great sounding music, "Shangrila," "Night in Tunisia," and "Overtura." The chills were running up and down my back, and the funny feeling was telling me something. No, it wasn't because I was cold either. I just had a feeling that they were going to do well. They received a Division I, of course. If they hadn't, then the judges must have totally been out to lunch or better yet, sleeping on the job. There was no reason in the world why the band shouldn't have done well.

Back in Martinsville Grandma and Grandpa Mathews took us to Poe's for supper. Senior Anna and her parents came in after we did. Anna promptly informed us they placed second and achieved 76 points! Wow! My first reaction or statement was "They are going to state. I can feel it in my bones." My funny feeling was right, wasn't it? I knew they were going to do well, and they did. Call it psychic, gut instinct or whatever, but I just knew something good was going to happen. I couldn't begin to tell you at that moment how proud I was to call myself an alumna. Before I walked away from Anna's table, her mom complimented me on my letter to the editor, and I promptly thanked her. Maybe my written words had meant something to the band. I would at least like to think so.

On Tuesday Mom called me at college and said if Saturday had been regional the Marching Arties would have gone to state. So cool! They were third of *all* Class A bands in the state. That was unbelievable! Now I was even prouder of them. Without much debate, Mom agreed to go with me to see them at regional in two weeks.

On Thursday before regional, Mom picked me up from my dormitory so I could see band practice one last time. I hated to miss class on that Friday, but oh, well. Band was more important at that moment than some boring psych class.

After practice that evening, juniors Glenda and Kathy asked me how the band looked.

I answered, "You looked good."

On Saturday, October 17, the band's do-or-die contest happened at Columbus East High School. I think half of the Class of 1987 was there to cheer the band on. Mrs. B and Mr. B's parents along with the newest addition to the family, Andrew, were also in attendance. By the way, Andrew was very cute.

As Mom and I sat down, Mrs. B said, "Oh, the Mathewses are sitting in front of us."

When the band marched onto the field, Roger and a couple of others yelled such things as, "Go Martinsville!" and, "Go Mr. B!" Mr. B turned around and smiled ear to ear.

Mrs. B said, "Well, at least you got a smile out of him."

I guess Mr. B was pretty nervous about the whole situation. Gees, who wouldn't be? His band was rated third in the state. If they didn't perform as well as they had two weeks before, then they would sit at home the following week instead of going to state finals. Who would want to do that? Here was the band's chance to finally make it to state finals. Yippee!

I thought the band looked great, totally awesome. There was no way they weren't going to state. In fact, my funny feeling returned, and I thought for sure I would be going to the Hoosier Dome the following week. My feeling was half right. They did earn a Division I but missed out on going to state. They had to be close, though, didn't they? I get really upset at these bands that get to go to state every year just because of their name. That's not fair to the other bands that are finally doing well enough.

My point is proved three days later when Mom called me at college and told me some bad news. The band placed sixth. Wow. If they had been in the north regional, they would have gone to state. Darn, how I hated the way ISSMA divides the state to determine which regional site the bands will compete. That is just so unfair. Mom's letter came the next day, and I still say they should have gone to state. They scored 83.2 points. Incredible, that's all I can say. Even though I was disappointed in the way the judges decide who goes to state, I was still very proud of the Martinsville Marching Artesians, and they should have been proud of themselves.

I read in my brother's *Artesian Herald* about the band. Mr. B said something about beating only Martinsville's best. How true, Mr. B, how true. I was so proud of them that I wished I could have hugged each and every one of them. They made me feel proud to say I was once a part of them. By the way, Ben Davis won Class A for the fourth year in a row, and Center Grove was second. How sickening.

In 1988 I still continued following the band by going to watch practices and supporting them in any way I could. Like Mr. B had done in the past few years, the band performed their state fair show for the parents and community. I, of course, went to see how the show looked before the big day the following week. They didn't look too bad, but then again I was standing at the same level they were so I really couldn't see how the forms looked from above. I stood right below Mr. B's ladder, and when he got down the first time the band finished the show, he grabbed the megaphone.

He said, "Hi, Michele."

I returned the greeting. Always good to be recognized for your efforts, my effort being a huge supporter of the band.

On Tuesday, August 23, as a tribute to my most favorite singer in the world, Rick Springfield, that is, on his birthday, the band once again competed at the Indiana State Fair Band Day. They made the Sweet 16 easily. I listened to the finals on WCBK that evening when I heard Martinsville was fifth and Richmond won first place.

The only thing I could think of was how those directors were going to lose their hair. Mr. B and Mr. Harris had promised the band, like they had the last three years, to get a flat top haircut if the band placed in the Top 5.

A couple of days later I went to see Mr. B and gave him an article from the *Indianapolis News*. He seemed very please to get it. I was curious to see how his haircut turned out. His hair was really short in the back but not as bad as I thought it would be. Maybe he had forbid them to cut it really short, or maybe whoever did it took pity on the guys and decided they didn't really want to cut off all of Mr. B's and Mr. H's hair.

In late September I sent a letter to the editor about the band and wished I hadn't done that when I found out they weren't doing very well. For some reason I just thought maybe it would help out and give them the pep they needed to excel and do the best they could. Besides, I could be very persuasive when I wrote something, much better than the verbal me.

The Friday before district, I went to see Mr. B and asked him what time the band performed. His attitude told me he didn't seem very hopeful. I only hoped they got out of district. Do you know how awful that would have been if they hadn't at least done that? Mom and I planned on going to district at Southport, but at 10:30 A.M. the contest was postponed because of rain to the next week. I was glad because I was afraid Mom wouldn't go in the rain, and they would have the contest anyway.

We ended up going the next week. Martinsville looked good other than a couple of missing people, in my opinion, but maybe it was because they ended up with an extra week of practice. Center Grove's show made me sick. I placed bets they would finally dethrone Ben Davis at state finals. The band did get a Division I, and they were a happy group of kids to say the least. Getting a Division I was always a good thing; at least then you had made it to regional.

I watched the band's last practice before regional. As they practiced on the football field, I sat on the bleachers close to the top of the press box freezing my you-know-what off. Toward the end of practice, Mr. B quickly walked down the bleachers and talked to the band, a pep talk trying to get them to run through the show as though they were really competing.

Mr. Harris came up the bleachers and said, "Hello."

When Mr. B returned, he said, "Hi, Michele."

On Friday I went to visit Mr. B at school. I gave him a black and white picture of the band I had developed in one of my journalism classes at IU and showed him the pictures I had taken at district, which he told me were good. He started playing 20 questions with me about school asking me how it was, if it was fun, where I was living (He said he had dated someone who had lived in Briscoe, the dorm where I lived.), and how Mom and Dad were.

I answered him as completely as honestly as I could because if the truth be known, I wanted to be living at home and commuting to IU so that I could see the band even more. I know this sounds crazy, but I knew in my heart that this band could make it to state. I could live my own dream, my dream of seeing them get to state finals, through the band, and if I was there, then I could say I was a part of it.

"Are you going tomorrow?" asked Mr. B.

"I want to go, but I don't have ride," I said.

"There will be extra room in the van if you want to go," he said.

I started to leave and then asked, "What time are you leaving?" Sure, why not? He made the offer, and since I wanted to go really bad, I needed to take him up on his offer.

I went to the last home football game since it was senior night. After the game, I found Mr. B in his office and told him, "I would like to take you up on your offer."

I had asked Mom if I could go. I don't know why I asked. Heck, I was over 18. I could do whatever I wanted. I guess I should have told her I was going; that was common courtesy since I was still living at home part of the time. Rule #34: always let me know when you're not going to be here for meals so that I don't prepare food and then no one is here to eat it. I could actually hear Mom's voice saying that to me when Mr. B had asked if I wanted a ride. I couldn't believe Mr. B had asked me to go like that. Maybe he was feeling sorry for me because he knew how much I was coming over to watch band practices and he also knew how much I still wanted to be a part of them, or maybe he was just trying to be a nice guy. Whatever his reason, I was truly glad he offered to let me ride with them.

On Saturday, October 15, the band competed in the ISSMA Regional at Bedford North Lawrence High School. I arrived at the high school to catch my ride to the contest at a little after 11 A.M. The students and two fathers were loading instruments onto the truck.

Mr. Harris asked, "How are you?"

"I'm fine," I said.

We left at 11:30 just like Mr. B said we would. Once I was in Mr. B's van with the three men, Mr. B, Mr. Harris, and Dan Flynn, the color guard instructor, Mr. B introduced me to Dan.

Mr. B said, "Dan, I don't believe you have met Michele."

Dan shook my hand and said, "Nice to meet you."

Mr. B said, "She graduated two years ago, right?"

I said, "Yeah."

Mr. H said, "She's a band addict. She's got little round things with "b's" on them in her blood."

Dan asked me if I played bass drum.

"No," I said, "clarinet."

Mr. H said, "Yeah, those would get stuck."

Since I didn't really have anyone to sit with in the bleachers, I stayed with the band through warm-ups and performance by standing on the sideline. I was so proud of them when they received a first division. Last week they scored a 60.5 and sixth out of six bands at district, and this week they achieved a 72.85 and eighth out of 14 bands. They beat all of the bands except Center Grove that had beaten them last week! How exciting! I was so darn proud of them.

An idea came to me. Whoa! Look out when I get ideas in my head. Sometimes I get a little dangerous. I decided I wanted to help with band next year if Mr. B would have me. My only problem was I wasn't sure I had enough courage to ask him.

On the way home Mr. H said his sister was organizing an alumni association for the band. Mr. B asked if I would help with publicity, and I told him I would.

After we arrived back at the high school, I didn't get a chance to thank Mr. B for taking me. I decided to send the band a congrats card and wrote a note on the inside for the band and a separate note to Mr. B thanking him for taking me and informing him of my wish to help with drill next year. I know I took the chicken way out, but writing is a lot easier for me than talking. I was having a hard time letting go of marching band. It was my thing, and this band meant a lot to me.

Mom called me at school and told me Kokomo made state finals. That was twice in four years. How in the world are they doing that? I know they were working hard and were very determined.

I went to see Mr. B the following Friday to talk to him. He should have gotten my note and card by then. Can you believe he took the day off? Darn him! I wanted to give him some pictures.

A few days later I found out the state finals results. Ben Davis won Class A for the fifth year in a row, and Center Grove was second. Kokomo wasn't last; they were ninth. At least they had the opportunity to go to state finals. That was all I wanted to see Martinsville do. I didn't care if they were 10th; at least, they were there.

Two or three weeks later I finally got to see Mr. B. I gave him the copies of the district pictures I had taken.

"These pictures are good," Mr. B said.

I told him, "I have an idea to do a newsletter like the one Kokomo band did."

"It's a good idea when or if I had the time do it or someone to do it," he said.

He looked at me and smiled from ear to ear. I got the feeling I was about to be nominated for the job, which was what I was hoping would happen. I loved doing that sort of thing, and I was a perfectionist to boot.

He then asked, "Would you be interested in doing the newsletter?"

No hesitation from me, I said, "Yes."

"We started putting one out for the whole music department, but we needed to keep it going through second semester and through the summer for marching band," he said.

Two months later the first newsletter was done, and Mr. B was pleased with it.

Nothing much happened the rest of that school year other than the fact Mom made a comment to me about helping with band next year. She told me to ask Mr. B if I could go with the band to Band Day. I was so surprised. I didn't think she had even noticed how much I enjoyed being involved with the band. She could have knocked me over with a feather after that comment.

After I moved home to commute to IU halfway through my sophomore year, I would have even more time to watch practices and contests in the fall of 1989. I won't go into how much I hated dorm life. That would be another book, and it's certainly not important to what I am writing here.

About a week before Band Day, I planned on asking Mr. B if I could ride with the band, but he had several students in his office after practice. I didn't want to fight my way through to talk to him so I decided I would just wait.

The following night I went to watch practice and found out what they had done. Jesse, the senior drum major, moved to Florida because his dad was transferred. Anyway, the band collected money to fly him back here for Band Day. Stan, a 1988 graduate and a friend of Jesse's, called Jesse and told him, and I guess Jesse cried.

After band I followed Mr. B into his office and said, "I have a question."

He told me, "Throw it at me."

I did. "Could I ride with the band to Band Day?"

He said, "Yes, but you'll have to ride a bus."

"What time are you leaving?" I asked.

"Eight A.M.," he replied.

At 6:15 A.M. on Wednesday, August 16, I woke up tired but excited. I was probably more nervous than the band was; that was why I was so tired. I couldn't wind down enough to go to sleep. I only hoped that they would do well.

At the high school I got on bus #23 with the Whites as chaperones. Not a very exciting trip since we had made it at least once a year for the past several years.

Once we arrived at the fair, the band had to hurry during warm-ups because Mr. B hadn't allowed enough time. Oops. During their morning performance, I stood in the infield behind them and took pictures. They didn't look very good, but at awards they made it to the Sweet 16. Senior Larry, who played a sax solo, passed out because of the heat. He was okay, though, to perform in the evening. After awards, we went to Ponderosa for our annual lunch. As we stood outside waiting on another band to finish eating, Mr. B stood with some band members and me talking about how they would do in the evening. Mr. B told one student he thought they would make the Top 5.

I wanted to say, "I bet you place third," because my funny feeling told me they would, but I never said a word. I was afraid to say anything, and I'm not really sure why. Maybe it was because I wasn't being realistic, and I didn't want them laughing at me or getting their hopes up. I had a yellow pass I used to go into the grandstands and watch the evening performance so I could get a different view. They looked and sounded so great. If they didn't make top five this year, the judges must be blind.

After the awards were done, I was really wishing I had said my thought about being third. Do you want to know why? They did place third. How could I have not said anything when I had the chance? Anyway, those kids were so darn happy. Heck, you should have seen me after their performance. I ran most of the way back to the buses. I wanted to scream at the top of my lungs that I thought they were going to do very well. Of course, you know I wouldn't really do that. You're reading about a chicken, remember? It was the highest placing in Martinsville's history.

When we got back to just outside of town, the moving twinkies got a police escort from the 39 Bypass at State Road 67 to the high school where the parents sat honking their car horns. I can actually still hear the horns honking. They were very loud to say the least, and I bet all of the neighbors loved hearing them in the wee hours of the morning.

Three days later I went to a local sporting goods store and had a clerk print a shirt with the Marching Artesian logo and the word "alumna" on it. I wanted to show the world how proud I was to have once been a part of them. I wrote my annual letter to the editor early this year. I just wanted to share what I was feeling about their Band Day performance with the whole community.

Before the first field show contests of the season, an article about the band appeared in *The Martinsville Reporter*. I was flattered because the picture that accompanied the article was one I had taken at district the previous year. Mr. B must have given it to the paper.

Even though I didn't go to the contests, I found out at Winchester the band got fourth and best drum major, and at Plainfield they received second and best percussion. I didn't think this was too bad considering that they didn't know about half of the last song's drill. I guess I can't say too much about the contests since I really didn't see the band perform.

On Saturday, September 30, 1989, even though I wasn't feeling very well, Mom and I went to see the band at ISSMA District at Southport. They earned a Division I while Center Grove won all of the caption awards as well as Division I. I didn't think Center Grove looked all that wonderful, not compared to years past. However, with a name like Center Grove, they had to do well. I'm not trying to badmouth them by any means. They are good. It's just that I wish the judges would give the "little guys" a little credit and put some of them where they needed to be in scoring.

A little over a week later I visited Mr. B at school and gave him a set of pictures from district. He asked me if I thought they looked good. I could tell by the way he talked he was pleased with their performance. I asked him if I could ride with the band on Saturday. He said sure and told me they were leaving at 11:45 A.M. I hoped I felt all right so that I could go. I had been fighting with a sinus infection for a month or better.

The band's big day at ISSMA Regional arrived, and I had planned on going with them. However, I had to go to the doctor to see if I could get some different medicine. I had been coughing and really having a bad time shaking the infection. Mom didn't think I should go with the band. It would have been different if I had driven myself so that I wasn't dependent on Mr. B to get me home. I could leave whenever I wanted. I wanted to go so badly, but I knew that Mom was right as much as I hated to admit that fact.

The next day I listened to the Fall Foliage Festival parade on WCBK. A 1988 graduate and former band member announced that the Marching Artesians finished their season yesterday. My brother Sean said he heard they were one of the worst bands there. I couldn't see that at all, but then again since the announcer hadn't said how they had placed it made me really wonder how they had finished. The only good news to come out of this ISSMA thing was that Ben Davis finally got beat by Center Grove, you know the band I didn't like at all.

I guess it just goes to show you that if you aren't a rich and or don't have a name like Ben Davis or Center Grove you might as well just do this for fun because you'll never make it to state finals without a big fancy name. I'm not directing this at either of these two bands; they are great bands, as I mentioned above a few paragraphs ago. I just wish the system was different so that the little guys like Martinsville have a chance to prove themselves. Martinsville doesn't get a lot of support from the community once Band Day is over, and that sucks. Sorry, I don't really like to use a word like that, but it's the only one that fits the situation, the simplest way to say it. Martinsville also doesn't get much money from the school system either, which doesn't help the situation at all. Then again many extracurricular programs didn't get a lot of funding, and that is really a shame. The kids need something to do. They need things like marching band to give them something to do. You know even maybe keep them out of a gang since there seems to be more and more of them.

There's not too much more to say during this transitional period for me, only that things in my dreary life began to change for the best. If someone had asked me today what the turning point in my life was, I would have to say what happened in the fall of 1990.

♫

Chapter 8

As I have already alluded, things couldn't have gotten any better for me than in the fall of 1990. Through working with Wendy's, Stephanie, a 1989 graduate, and I became what I would call good friends. I think it was this association that helped me open up more to people. I had always been shy, but the moving my family had done had made me even quieter and reserved when communicating with other kids. This would have played a significant role in what happened by the end of August. Keeping you in suspense? I sure hope so.

Let me back up a little bit. I continued what I had been doing for the past three summers, watching the band practice. During one of the first practices Mr. B asked me if the band would make Top 5 at the state fair, and I told him I didn't know. I asked him if the band was smaller than last year's. He said it was probably a little bigger. It didn't really look like it to me, but who was I to argue? He was the band director. He ought to know if the band was bigger, smaller or the same size as last year's band.

The next night I skipped the boring summer school class I was taking and went to watch band practice. You're probably thinking right about now that I was obsessed with band. I would have to say you are probably right. When you didn't have anything else to do, you did what you could find. Anyway, I took five or six pictures of the band so I could get a roll of film out of my camera.

Mr. B asked me, "Do you want to work with the pit?"

"I don't know anything about that," I replied.

He said, "Oh, drats."

A couple of weeks before Band Day, Stephanie and I talked to Mr. B at practice. He told the band that if they win at Band Day then a band mom with very long hair, reaching to her buttocks, would cut her hair.

A week later I stopped to watch the band on my way home at 8:45 P.M. Several people, including Stephanie, Lynn, Mrs. B and their two kids, were there. Stephanie was holding the newest addition to the Brenneman family, Hannah Michele, who was born four months before. The middle name was pretty cool if I do say so myself. To this day, I still wonder where the Brennemans came up this name. Was it really because of me? Stephanie and I made the decision to go watch Band Day, and I would do the driving.

The day before Band Day I watched the band's last practice. They sure looked good. I just hoped they would do well the following day. I called Stephanie when I got home to see if she got our tickets. They were sold out of the morning show, but she did get evening tickets. We were almost set then.

On Wednesday, August 15, I picked Stephanie up at 6:45 A.M., and then we got donuts at the bakery since neither of us had eaten breakfast. We got in line for the caravan but didn't leave until 7:30. Somehow, I don't know how I managed it, but we followed the buses into the infield because the guys directing traffic told us to follow the buses. Usually the infield is only for the buses and staff vehicles. That made it good for us because we would be close to the band and because we had a cooler for food and drinks in the trunk of my car. Stephanie and I each bought a program, and Kari Jones, Lynn's sister, was on the cover. Stephanie and I ran to show Kari and her mom. Imagine how Kari must have felt having her picture on the cover of a program that was seen by thousands of people. I should have asked for her autograph.

Stephanie and I bought our morning show tickets and found our seats. The band didn't look too bad, but they could have done better. As we were watching the bands, I glanced at the people moving around on the bleachers and saw a man in a Haworth band jacket. I kept looking to see who it was because all I could see was his back. You'll never guess who it was! Mr. Haggard, my former director! He hadn't changed one bit. He was working with the Jay County Band; I found his name in the program. As the morning awards were getting ready to be announced, Stephanie and I walked down to be with the Martinsville crowd in the bleachers. (They were in the opposite end from us.) Mr. B was sitting and looking so relaxed that I decided to take a picture of him. The band made the Sweet 16 once again. Stephanie and I ate lunch or supper; it was between 3 and 4 when we got to eat. After we finished eating, we goofed around until the band returned from Ponderosa and the church where they went annually to rest.

At 7 P.M. Stephanie and I ventured around among the band as they prepared for the evening performance. We talked to Laura, senior and only drum major, and then took turns shaking her hand and wishing her good luck. I couldn't believe how much better they looked. Well, they placed 7th. I thought for sure they would get top five. The thing that really ticked me off is a band like Concord High School from South Bend. They supposedly learned their show in 11 hours and beat us. All they did was march on the track's field in a box, stand to play, maybe move around, and then march off. They didn't even wear uniforms, just T-shirts and shorts. Do you know why they beat us? They are a state finalist in Class B pretty consistently.

When Stephanie and I got back to the buses, Laura was upset. We tried to make her feel better.

I told Laura, "You guys were so much better in the evening."

She agreed and said, "It was like two different bands."

Mr. B told the whole band, "I can't help it if the judges were blind."

Stephanie and I were behind Mr. B's van all the way home. We arrived back in Martinsville at 12:45 A.M. The Arty fire truck, the biggest fire truck, led us through town. Stephanie and I took turns honking my car horn.

At the high school, I yelled, "Bye, James," out Stephanie's open window. I don't honestly know what possessed me to do that other than the fact I had drank three or four cans of Mountain Dew. Mountain Dew will do that to me, make me as hyper as ever. Besides, I really didn't see any harm in calling James by his first name because Stephanie had told me earlier that Mr. B had told her to call him James.

Okay, here's the moment you've been waiting for. On Friday, August 24, one of the most important events in my life happened; my dream finally came true.

After picking up pictures up from Band Day a couple of days before, I went to visit Mr. B during his prep the last class of the day. I gave him the pictures. He looked at them and told me they were good pictures.

He asked me if I was living at home.

I said, "Yes."

He was wondering if I would want to help with the band since I was over there every night anyway.

I said, "Yes," in such a way that he would think I was so excited I could hardly stand it. How could I not say yes? This was what I had been dreaming about since I had graduated from high school and most especially since that day I had ridden in Mr. B's van to regional. I want this band to go to state. After I gave Mr. B my answer, he showed me the drill on his computer he had written himself. Not too shabby.

On Tuesday, August 28, I went to band practice, not as a supporter, but as a staff member for the very first time. Staff member were two words that had to grow on me. I couldn't believe I was finally one. Now my only worry was how the kids would act toward me. Would they respect me and look at me as an adult? I wasn't that much older than the seniors, only about three to four years older.

By the end of the second practice I attended, I decided I really did like working with the band. I was getting used to the kids, and I think they were getting used to me.

A week later that practice didn't start out very well. In fact, Mr. B was yelling at them when I got there. They did learn all of the middle song drill, and I thought they looked pretty decent. A couple of kids in my line consisting of clarinets, the instrument of choice, and the flutes asked me questions about what band I was in, and I had to tell them Martinsville, of course.

The next night was a home football game. I went over and hoped to get into the football game with the band so I didn't have to pay to get in. The band performed their state fair show, and actually looked great, almost as good as the night show a few weeks before.

As we continued cleaning and working on the drill, the first contests were approaching fast. We practiced on the Saturday a week before the first contest; however, many of the kids weren't there. That doesn't help to polish a show when holes exist. It's too hard for the kids on either side of the hole to judge how much space to leave, and most especially when they are freshman.

At the beginning of practice on Tuesday before the first contest, Mr. B said something like "no one should be talking except Kenny, Michele and Jackie if she's out there." He actually made me feel important. Wow! How great it felt to be a "staff member!"

At the other practice of that week, Mr. B made the staff wear those goofy headsets, like walkie talkies. I heard some interesting words from him. In a way, I was grateful to Mr. B because he made me feel like I was really staff. He told me to yell at the flutes for getting their intervals too small. The kids started yelling at me so they could ask questions. That made me feel even more important; one less thing to worry about because they did respect me enough to ask for help. The closer, especially during a straight line, had kids missing the first step, and they were hardly playing the music.

Mr. B asked me, "Are they looking better?"

I told him, "No."

Then he blew up at the kids and said, "Now play the damn thing."

Wow, Mr. B, you surprised me. I knew how frustrating it was when the kids didn't care, which obviously they didn't at this practice. This band just didn't seem to have the drive that the previous year's band had. I couldn't quite put my finger on it.

Our first weekend of band contests turned out not too badly. At Center Grove High School, they scored 43 and placed fifth out of 11

74

bands and seventh out of 13 overall, and at Hamilton Southeastern High School, located up by Noblesville, they increased their score by six points and placed second out of two bands. Things looked grim for the Marching Artesians.

On the way home from the second contest, Mr. B, since I still couldn't bring myself to call him James to his face, told Mrs. B that he doesn't think we would have to worry about regional. I had so much fun even though it was such a long day. It sure is different riding in the van and listening to Mr. B talk about the band. All I could think about on the way home was how much I wanted to help next year. I would love to go to Florida with them. They would go over spring break to Disney World. Wouldn't that be exciting, especially since I haven't been to Disney World in 15 years?

When we got back to the high school, I thanked them for taking me.

He said, "Anytime."

"Don't say that again because I might need a ride next week," I told him.

He said that would be okay.

The following week at practice Laura said a few words to the band. Then Mr. B did. I was worried about what I had said in a letter to the editor that I sent to *The Martinsville Reporter.* I didn't want to say something that might have made him mad. However, everything he said to the band were some of the things I wrote in the letter. I was so relieved about that. Wouldn't that have been awful if I had made him mad and then he would "fire" me? He also told them unless 50 people joined band next year all he would do is Band Day.

"I am sick and tired of competing against huge bands like Center Grove and Ben Davis," Mr. B said.

The second practice of that week was fine. Mr. B made the kids run through the show about three or four times. My letter wasn't in that evening's paper as I glanced through it when I got home from practice. My funny feeling told me something wasn't right. Were the kids really not going to make it to regional? Would we be sitting at home that weekend? In fact, I was beginning to get a little scared for these kids. As much as I hated to even think about it, I really didn't think they would make it out of district and advance to regional. Something was missing from this band that I had never seen happen before. I think it was because there wasn't any senior leadership, no one to get the band united and fired up.

On Saturday, September 29, 1990, ISSMA District came and went leaving things happening the way we thought they would. At 4 P.M. that day the Marching Artesians found out they earned a second division. As the staff stood around the buses waiting on the kids to put away instruments and change clothes, Mr. B told Mrs. B that he knew all week the band wouldn't make it to regional.

We still went to the Ben Davis contest that evening, and some of the kids I saw before we left didn't seem that upset. Maybe they knew deep down, too, that they wouldn't be going to regional. In fact, they wanted to go to the other contest.

Mr. B turned the kids loose in the Greenwood Mall to eat supper and kill time. I hung out with the Brennemans since they didn't care. Would you believe that we dropped our points at Ben Davis? How could that happen? We received a 57.50 at district and a 50 at Ben Davis.

Back at Martinsville High School I asked Mr. B, "Are we going to have practice on Tuesday?"

He said, "Yes, they have to improve."

The following day I was still pretty tired. Helping the band was a great experience for me, and it sure kept me busy. I mean I love this band, and that is the only way to say it. I wanted this band to go to state so badly that it wasn't funny. Do I sound crazy to want to help with band like this? In fact, now that I have helped, I realized what I wanted to do as a career. I wanted to be a teacher. Working with these kids and becoming a more outgoing person, I realized that I wanted to teach. I loved the way the kids would ask me questions and the way I could teach them what I knew. What a great feeling that was!

I went to band practice the following Tuesday. Mr. B lectured for around a half hour about how he is going to change the band system next year. He had some good ideas, and I hoped one of them worked.

He ended his lectures by showing the tapes from each of the contests on Saturday. They practiced the last two hours.

A junior clarinet player asked me, "Are you going to help next year?"

I said, "I would like to, but it's up to Mr. B." If he did say yes, then I planned on asking if I could come to the band banquet and if I could order a staff jacket. I was really feeling like staff now.

Later, Mr. B apparently forgot to take his drill charts to the field.

When we got to the closer, he got his megaphone, and in front of the whole band, he said, "Michele Mathews, do you have charts?"

I was standing only a few feet away from him. Oh, well, it made me feel important.

During our last practice another clarinet player asked me if I would help next year. I told her the same thing I told the other girl on Tuesday.

My letter to the editor was finally in the paper as I glanced at it before practice. A lot of good it would do now. It should have been in about a week sooner. Mr. B told me it was a "nice letter."

Before the football game I arrived at the high school so I could talk to Mr. B. without students interrupting.

I asked, "Would you care if I came to the band banquet?"

He answered, "You're more than welcome. In fact, more than some of the rest of them."

I said, "A couple of kids have come up to me and asked if I am going to help next year. I told them it would be up to you."

He said, "Do you want to help?"

I said, "Well, I would like to."

I don't really remember his exact words, but the answer was "yes." I then asked about ordering a band jacket, and he took my name and size. Well, if everything worked out the way I hoped it would in my life, I would be staff the following year.

Even though we didn't make it to regional, the band had a contest on the following Saturday at Westfield High School close to Kokomo. I was the only one to ride with Brennemans, and we really didn't say too much. Mr. B told Mrs. B as he got in the van to leave for the contest that none of his staff showed up except me; he seemed a little frustrated. The band got third out of four bands in their class. First place went to Columbus North, second to Lawrence Central, and fourth to Marion. We were also second in drum major, color guard and general effect. I could tell you the best part about going to this contest, but I'll spare Mr. B the embarrassment.

At the last home football game I asked Mr. B if I could go with the group of students and him to state finals. He told me to sign up on the band room door. I asked him what time they were leaving, and he said he didn't know. I asked if he could call me, but he told me he would tell me at the band banquet. However, that wouldn't work since the banquet was after state. He decided he would call me.

A few days later I took Mr. B the pictures of the band in the Fall Foliage parade. He thanked me for them.

I asked him if they were still going to state on Saturday, and he said, "Yes."

I asked him what time they were leaving, and he said, "Noon." Then he was glad I had stopped by because he probably would have forgotten to call me.

Because he had two people in his office, I decided to leave and said, "See ya Saturday."

He looked at me kind of funny and said, "Okay."

On Saturday, October 27, I attended my first state band finals contest along with Mr. B and 17 band students. We shouldn't have gone that early because we arrived just as the second Class C band performed meaning we had the rest of the C bands and then the B and A bands to watch. That's way too much time to sit on hard metal bleachers. By the time the Class A awards started, I could no longer feel my buttocks; they were numb. Carmel won Class A, the class Martinsville competed in. The audience stood up and applauded after they were done, totally awesome show. The other bands in Class A included Center Grove, second and our biggest competitor, Lawrence North – third, and Ben Davis – fourth. That last band was a surprise. They had won so many years in a row, and for them to be fourth must have been a shock.

On Monday, October 29, at the band banquet, Mr. B was staring at something and probably thinking how much he wished his band would make state finals or maybe he was just bummed because of how horrible the band had done that year.

He said, "Hi, Michele," and told me I could sit at the staff table.

Before the awards were handed out, Mr. B borrowed my black pen to sign a first year award he had forgotten to do.

He told me, "Make yourself useful, Michele," by helping him unwrap the awards. That was weird seeing who was going to win the awards before the students even knew.

During the serious awards at some point, Mr. B thanked his staff. He made Jackie and me stand up to be recognized and applauded. Mr. B smiled at me as I stood up after his introduction. I just hoped he wouldn't change his mind about me helping next year.

After the awards I had to ask for my pen back.

"Have you ordered band jackets yet?" I asked him.

He said, "I'm still getting orders. Have you filled out an order form?"

I told him no.

He told me to call him.

I decided just to send him my name and size so he had it on paper. That band jacket was extremely important to me. I would be recognized as a staff member and not a student as I knew I would be since I looked younger than I actually was.

On the night of Monday, November 12, I could tell something bad had happened when I arrived home 10 minutes late; my class had run over. Mom and Dad were eating supper and not saying much. Mom stated I was late. I went to my room, put my book bag down and returned to the kitchen for supper.

As I filled my glass with Kool-aid, Mom informed me Alex, a junior in band was killed the previous night coming home from his girlfriend's house.

My first gut reaction was, "Oh, my gosh." I couldn't say anything else; I didn't even know what to say. Mom seemed to be really upset.

The accident happened on State Road 44 near Hess Road, a very bad place along that road. Alex was thrown from the vehicle. That was all the details I would prefer to give regarding the actual accident, so tragic. Alex was in marching band playing one of the keyboards, and he sacked groceries at Marsh. I didn't really know him that well even though I did help with band. Alex always seemed so friendly.

The next day I thought about going to the viewing for Alex, but it was late by the time I got back from class and run my errands. According to the local newspaper, memorial contributions were to be made to the jazz band, in which Alex was also involved. Mr. B planned to purchase a piano in Alex's honor.

On Wednesday Alex was buried with his saxophone, a decision his parents made, according to a couple of women and band moms I worked with. Alex had planned on becoming a composer so some of the music he had written was played at the funeral. I heard the music was awesome.

You don't know how precious life is until you lose someone like Alex. I feel so sorry for his parents and anybody who was really close to him. He will be sadly missed. I am sure of that.

NOTE: The piano in Alex's honor was a black Baldwin. Mr. B dedicated it at a jazz band concert in March.

♫

Chapter 9

The 1991 marching season got a little better for the kids and a lot better for me. I didn't know I could have had so much fun helping with the band. Anyway, the season started the first of June during the introductory week. It was funny/strange how I found out.

I was sitting at Wendy's, the awful place where I worked at the time, eating supper with a co-worker when I thought I saw Brennemans' van at the drive-through window. I was right. I waved at them as Mr. B drove past the window where I sat. He stopped, backed up and motioned for me. I went outside where he told me band starts Monday at 6 P.M. As he drove away, I felt as if I were floating in the white, fluffy clouds; I was so very happy.

That four-day week of band was a little better than the way we had ended the previous year. Mr. B seemed very determined to make this band good, if not great. They worked on marching for a little while.

Mr. B asked me, "Is the band going to be very good?"

I said, "Yeah, better than last year."

He just laughed. Anything had to be better than last year, didn't it? We surely couldn't get any worse. Otherwise, we might as well give up now.

By Thursday the music and early marching look very good. I hoped they would do as well as I thought they would. I wanted this band to go to state so badly.

"Did you order me a band jacket?" I asked Mr. B.

He didn't say anything for a couple of minutes and then said, "I guess not, but we'll probably order again later."

I was disappointed; I was really looking forward to wearing a staff jacket this fall.

Once band started in July, I could only think about how much I wanted this band to do better than last year and go to state. There were a few students who just didn't even seem to be trying to march, but at least it wasn't like last year when it seemed as though it was half or more of the band.

On Saturday, July 27, Mr. B had a cookout at his house for the staff and a few parents, those who usually do the most. I arrived early, but that was okay because the extra time allowed me to talk Mr. B into going to the Kokomo Invitational the week before district. I think I succeeded. Dan and I had a chat about Harold Gallant, the man who wrote Kokomo's drill as well as ours that year.

During band camp I finally decided I could call Mr. B James, although most of the time I wouldn't call him anything. In fact, I didn't get the courage to call him James to his face for one and a half years. I didn't feel right in calling him by his first name, especially since he had been my teacher. Anyway, I took the week off from Wendy's, major burnout was beginning and I desperately needed a break so I could spend the time helping with band camp.

On the first day the weather was sunny and 80 or 85 degrees. We got a lot done. James and Eric seemed very pleased with how easy the field show went together. Lunches with the staff were interesting. This was the first year I ate lunch with them, and boy, I didn't want to miss anything, too much fun to miss. Ken Roe, newest staff member, kept us laughing in stitches. Ken, an intelligent and witty guy, wrote music and played trumpet and was a doctoral student at IU. With Ken there was never a dull moment. Let me give you an example.

One lunch he said something to James as they ate sandwiches from Subway. I understood what he had said, but James didn't understand until Ken had said it two or three times. Ken said the huge wrap around the sandwich is for fallout. That was why the paper was so huge. So funny he was. All I could think about was how weird it was to be with staff. You sure got treated differently, and you got a whole different perspective on James.

On the last day of band camp, the kids seemed to be tired. I knew I was. I had to go to Bloomington to pick up my grade for my last speech, a class I was taking in order to earn my teaching license. I made it back just in time for squad competitions at 2:30 P.M. It was so incredibly hot outside that I didn't know if I would make it or not. James sent freshmen inside to get chairs, and I went to get some water before I passed out.

During our two-hour break for supper, the staff went to Harris' where we filled our tummies with chili cheese dogs, potato chips, Mrs. H's infamous cheesy dip, and fabulous desserts.

The 6 to 8 P.M. rehearsal wasn't too bad, but you could tell the kids were thinking of the later activities: the talent show, dance, and overnight. After the dance was over at midnight or 1 A.M., Larry, a band alumnus, James and I discussed various subjects as we hung around James's office. When the kids finally settled down at 2:30 A.M., I left for home.

The next week at band practice James, Dan and I were in the office when James said something about being tired, and Dan wondered why. I was sitting down, and they were both standing up and looking at me. James pointed at me and said he left school at 2:30 A.M. Saturday, got up at 6:30 to prepare for his church softball tourney game at 8:30 and played in four or five games.

James gave the band one of his infamous lectures because rehearsal wasn't going very well.

The day before Band Day as the band prepared for a dress rehearsal for the annual Red and Blue games, I had many compliments on my new look, my new glasses. (I had been having trouble wearing my contacts and I couldn't see with my old glasses.) Larry, Ken, James and I were in the band office.

Ken told all of us, "Michele is in disguise tonight."

Like I said earlier, there was never a dull moment with Ken around.

The band marched at the annual Red and Blue game and looked pretty good considering the grass was a foot high. Why don't you cut the grass once in a while? It sure would make it easier for those poor kids to march.

On Wednesday, August 14, the annual Band Day arrived. I rode with James, Eric, and Larry in the staff van, Harris' new one. We had fun with Eric and his little writing board. He had had his mouth wired shut to fix a major dental problem. We ended up marching in the 12th position instead of 13th, a band had dropped out of competition. The Marching Artesians looked and sounded good, but they still got ninth in the morning show. Competition was stopped at one point due to the lightning in the area.

After our band's performance James had to go to the hospital with a girl who didn't take her heart medicine. I stayed at the fair with Tracey, Eric and his wife, while the band went to Ponderosa, one of the things I looked forward to besides the band winning big. We finally ended up back with the band at "our" church on 38th Street, our resting area before the evening show, or actually it was the McDonald's across the street where we ate supper.

For the Sweet 16 in the evening, I followed the band to warm-ups. I told Ken I would carry the tuners, and James asked me to take his megaphone. I had my funny feeling back. The band looked so good. They placed fifth, which explained my funny feeling! Not only did James remember to put my name in this year's program, but my picture would be in the following year's program. How cool was that! As a top five finisher, the staff and drum majors got their picture taken for the next year's program. We finally got home at 1 A.M.

I went to Wal-mart the next day and dropped off a roll of film from Band Day. In the Bloomington *Herald-Times* paper box outside the store, I saw a color picture of our band on the front page and bought a copy of it on my way out of the store. As I was looking at it, I heard a voice say something about buying a paper. I looked up, and it was Tracey. She bought one, too, after I told her there were only two copies left. Now what would I do? I didn't know what to do with myself since we didn't have practice for close to a week.

Once school started, practices continued. I gave James a set of Band Day pictures. A band mom was in the office before practice started one night.

James told her, "The band had to get money soon." He looked at me and said, "Otherwise, it will just be Michele and me like last year."

That comment surprised me, but he was right. The school was paying him, and I was volunteering my time.

During fundamentals, he said, "Michele, I want you to hang out with the woodwinds and holler at them if they aren't standing still at attention."

Boy! I felt so important! No problem, boss. They needed to learn to stand still. Some of them couldn't stand still if their life depended on it.

James, Rod, who was another staff member, and I were walking from the band room through the school to the football field, which was out the opposite end of the building. James told us about a mellophone player who had evidently quit. She marched at state fair and hadn't been seen since. James wasn't happy to say the least. That only created a hole in the show, and holes weren't a good thing because the member on each side of it must maintain that hole. Otherwise, it looked like the intervals were wrong.

On Saturday, August 31, Larry, Eric's wife and daughter, Eric, James, and I rode in Brennemans' van to the Hoosier Dome game where the band performed at half time.

On the way home James and Eric discussed how far 75 miles were. They had decided to walk home from the Dome if the band made it to state. A long way was all I could think of. I sure wouldn't want to walk all the way home.

The following week's rehearsals were pretty good. The kids learned two new drill charts for their last song. I was beginning to hate my name because the kids kept yelling for me. However, on the other hand, at least they boosted my confidence. I was building a huge respect for them and them for me. James, Todd, another alumnus volunteering to help, and I were the only three there until Rod joined us later. Oh, well, I was having fun.

I told James, "Bye," when we got back to the band office.

He said, "Thanks, Michele."

I think he really enjoyed having help and not having to do this by himself. He probably didn't know what he would do without his alumni. Without us he would have been doing this by himself.

At the first home football game, I stood with James, Larry, and Rod at the railing on the bleachers down in front of the band. Tracey came with the kids. When the band performed, I moved up to sit with them on the bleachers. A 1988 graduate announced my name as staff, which was neat and made me feel even more important. Can you feel my head getting bigger? After the band finished its halftime performance and settled back on the bleachers, James came up the bleachers and sat down on the other side of Tracey.

He asked us, "How did the band look?"

I told him, "Pretty good except I could hardly hear them some of the time."

In James's office after the game, Larry and I looked at the last four drill charts of the show.

James told us, "The band ought to get either third or fourth out of nine bands at New Castle."

Kokomo and Huntington North high schools, the two schools I almost attended, would be there.

At practice the next week, a freshman clarinet-turned-tuba, claimed to supposedly know more than me about the drill, and I was the one with the charts in my hands. I was trying to defend the couple of kids who tried to tell her she was wrong. I should have made her run for back talking me. I really kicked myself later for not doing that. If I am going to be a teacher, the kids needed to listen to me now, and I needed to enforce it. James thanked me again for helping even though I really didn't do much.

James decided to change the practice schedule for the next week because he said the intensity went down from 8 to 9 P.M. so he hoped the change would help. Practices on Mondays and Wednesdays were 2:30-4:15 P.M. and on Tuesdays and Thursdays 6-8 P.M. I liked the idea, but I had class all day on Monday and most of Wednesday so I would miss most of practice.

On the Thursday practice before the first contest, we worked on the third, or last, song again. A junior clarinet player named Lilly tried to make it look as though I wasn't doing my job.

She told James, "Michele hadn't really placed us in the correct position."

You must understand the charts for this song were missing two clarinets so we had to improvise. Well, anyway, James asked me if I had, and I said I did. Pay attention, Lilly, would you?

On the homecoming football game night as the uniformed kids walked from the band room to the parking lot outside, James told them to stay zipped at all times or something like that. Eric and I looked at each other and started laughing.

"I wonder if he realizes what he just said," I said to Eric.

Eric went over to say something to James away from the kids. James began laughing and kept walking. When he had walked a few steps down the sidewalk on our way to the football field, James ended up bent over laughing hard. It was so very funny. Guess you had to be there, though.

On the day of the first contest, Saturday, September 21, I wasn't feeling that great and wasn't moving that fast. I did go to band practice at 3 P.M. but didn't do anything. James worked on the third song and ran through the show five or six times, which looked good the last time through.

On the way to the New Castle contest, James asked me how long it would take to get to Kokomo since he knew I had lived there, and I told him probably one and a half hours, maybe two hours by bus. The band didn't do as well we had hoped; they were fifth with 52.6 points. Huntington North was fourth, and Kokomo was second. I hoped we would beat them both. Mr. Murray still helped with Kokomo's band; he was on the sidelines when I watched them. When we got back to the high school, James, Eric, Larry and I (and some others, but I can't remember who) stood outside talking about the band, what we could do to improve.

The next week the band finally finished learning their show. I was in the office by myself looking at the agenda for the next Saturday when James came in and started talking to me. He said they got all but a few charts learned yesterday.

As I walked to the field, I heard a vehicle beside me. I looked over, and it was James wanting to give me a ride over to the football field.

That was a long walk, a walk I didn't want to have to do if I could avoid it. I didn't really do too much that week. James cleaned on the last song once they finished learning it.

After practice on Thursday, Dan, James and I sat in the office talking about the messed up way that ISSMA does the regional contest.

James said, "We could be the sixth or seventh best band in the state and still not go to state."

How true that was. Actually, remember when I was in Kokomo and that happened to that band? Had we been in the south, we would have made it to state finals instead of sitting at home that weekend.

On Saturday, September 28, I left at 10 A.M. for band practice and two contests. I rode over and back with James in his van to the field. Practice wasn't too bad until senior drum major Angie had to be taken to the hospital with back spasms. Her mom said she would try to get Angie to the contests. The band had a picnic before we left.

On our way to Kokomo, James kept asking me how much longer. It sure was weird to be on my old stomping grounds. I saw Kokomo with Mr. Murray on the sidelines again. We got second with a 55.85 behind Lawrence North. James was happy. I just hoped they could get a 60 at Westfield in the evening. Since James, Rod and Dan had stayed for the critique while Tracey and I waited in the van and the band went on, James asked me which way to go. We had come in what I would have called the back way so I told him how to go the other way.

When we got to Westfield for the second contest, James looked at the scores from Kokomo and talked to me about them. Instead of sitting in the bleachers, I stayed with the band when they went to warm-ups and performance. The band got third and scored better than I had hoped they would. They earned a 64! James was very happy to say the least. I even somehow managed to get my name in the programs at both places and my name read over the loudspeaker at Westfield.

I was feeling so inspired from yesterday that I decided to write a letter to the editor of the local newspaper like I had done for the last few years. It was just a way to hype the band up for next week's district contest. I just hoped the paper got the letter in before next Saturday.

When I got to the last practice before district, James had already gone to the football field. I didn't really help very much. When he ran big chunks of the show at a time, there wasn't much to do. After practice Rod, James and I talked about the band and Saturday's district contest. James hoped they would send us to Columbus, but they didn't.

On Friday, October 4, James practiced the band for a half hour before they went to the last home football game. Larry told me he liked my letter to the editor. Once the band was seated on the bleachers, I stood at the railing.

Eric saw me, pointed at me, patted me on the back and said, "That was a nice letter."

I said, "Thanks."

He said, "I'm going to cut it out and put it on my bulletin board."

The band looked good at halftime.

On Saturday, October 5, we left at 1:30 P.M. for Southport High School to compete in the ISSMA District contest. It had rained so there were puddles. As the band marched from warm-ups to the stadium where they performed, Eric stood on one side to keep the kids from falling into the ditch, and James stood on the other to avoid a puddle. I told James and the kids not push Mr. Harris in the ditch.

James said, "Yeah, go ahead and push Mr. Harris in."

I ended up taking pictures from the track. The band did get a Division I trophy. I received a hug from Dan as we stood on the track surrounding the football field listening to results. (We were the last band to perform so we just stayed instead of going back to the buses to put away instruments and change out of uniforms.)

When we arrived back at the buses after results, James came with the scores and wasn't at all happy. I asked what the scores were. He said Center Grove beat us by 11 points.

"Are you serious?" I asked.

He told me, "Our score was lower than last week. We got a 62."

I couldn't believe that. What in the world were the judges looking at? Maybe they weren't even watching our band as they performed. Who knows? We were home by 5:15 P.M., just in time for me to sit around and do nothing. Do you want to know how boring this town is? Well, nah, I had better not even say anything here. Besides, it would take too long.

The following week's practices weren't too bad. I rode over to the field with James in his van. He told me I would be in charge of woodwind horn positions, making sure each member was holding his/her instrument correctly.

On Thursday I picked up my pictures I had taken on Saturday and went to West Middle School where the band met in order to march downtown for the annual Fall Foliage Festival Appreciation Night.

In the school before we left for downtown, James said, "Hi, Michele," as he went around a corner.

I said, "Hi."

The band marched down the street to the downtown area, stood on a blocked off street and played through their show to their heart's content. Then the crowd applauded them, and they marched back to West Middle. No big deal.

After the band finished their performance downtown, James gave the kids time to get to the high school for the rest of practice. Once practice finally started at 6:45 P.M., James had me call a band parent whose child didn't show up at practice after she was downtown. I received no answer at her house. When I got back, James got upset with me because the clarinets were messed up.

As he went down the bleachers from the press box, he said looking at me sitting on the bleachers, "That's wrong, Michele."

I could tell he was angry by the tone in his voice. He didn't tell me what he wanted me to do. I couldn't help it he was the only paid director there. I couldn't help it I was gone for a few minutes to go make a phone call he wanted me to make; heck, I didn't even know what they were doing when I got back. Maybe if he paid me a little something I would work a little harder, but I didn't really expect to get paid. I was there to help a great band and gain some teaching experience. Besides, Harold Gallant, our drill writer, was there and gave James a few pointers. I really didn't think I was needed and wanted to hear what Harold was saying as he stood on the bleachers watching the band move through their show. James must have really been upset with me because he never even introduced Harold to me. On the other hand, I think he was upset with that girl, and I just happened to be the one he took his anger out on. I don't know. I'm not a shrink, though, so I could have been wrong.

On Saturday, October 12, I went to band practice a little bit before 4 P.M. and put pictures on James's desk from last week.

He said, "Michele, what are you doing tomorrow?"

I said, "Well, I was going to take my grandma to the parade."

He said, "How would you like to judge the marching bands?" (He was talking about the marching bands in the Fall Foliage Festival parade, the second biggest parade in Indiana.)

I said, "Sure." I just hoped Grandma understood why I couldn't take her to the parade.

At the Center Grove contest I ended up staying with the band through warm-ups and performance. It sure was cold, and the band showed that. I really didn't think they performed that well, or at least, I didn't get as excited as I had last week. I ended up helping Angie off the field. Her back was still bothering her, and she could hardly walk. James passed us and asked if everything was okay.

After I got Angie back to the buses, I walked back over to the field with James and Larry to see Castle and Center Grove perform. They were two of our biggest competitors. We placed fourth and scored 58. James was mad to say the least. Heck, why shouldn't he be? Our score kept going down. We were now below what they had scored at district and 12 points shy of getting a Division I at regional next week. That was a little ridiculous.

The next day downtown Dan, Rod and I judged the four bands in the FFF parade and managed to see the whole parade, including Brian Austin Greene from *Beverly Hills 90210*. That was so cool! It was one of my favorite shows at the time, and here I was sitting no more than maybe 15 feet from one of the leading stars. I was way too shy to go ask him for an autograph, but I did get a smile from him. That was even better than an autograph, although the autograph would have been nice, too.

Back at the high school, James found out that we perform at 3:17 P.M., right after break, next Saturday at regional. Dan said he heard it is rumored in Evansville, which was where we went, that we would make it to state. James laughed. I only hoped and prayed it was true.

The big day, or the do-or-die day as I always called it, was a fun day even though we didn't do as well as we hoped. The band ran through the show a couple of times at 8:30 A.M. on the parking lot before we left for ISSMA Regional at Evansville. In Brennemans' van, Larry, Dan, Jesse (remember him?) and I joined James and Tracey.

Since the journey was the longest one of the marching season, we stopped at the Executive Inn in Vincennes to use restrooms and eat our sack lunches. Because the road we needed to get us to the contest was closed, we were later getting to the contest. Once the kids were ready and in uniforms, I walked with James and our guides in front of the band to warm-ups and then to the field. After their performance I thought the band looked great, the best they had looked all year. Eric patted me on the back. I asked him how he thought they did. He thought they were great.

Well, we were disappointed when we learned we received a Division II, a score of 69.80, missing a Division I by two-tenths of a darn point. Can you believe that? The only good thing was we had improved our score greatly. At least, we were at regional instead of staying home like the year before.

After James talked to the kids, he decided to stop for supper at a Burger King down the street. Inside I sat with Larry, Dan, James and Tracey.

Tracey asked me, "Are you going to Florida next spring with the band?"

I told her, "I will have to see what my class schedule will be." I only hoped I could go especially after the day I had had today.

After hardly saying anything on the way down, we sure made up for it on the way home. We discussed music for the next year, Led Zeppelin, Pink Floyd, Beach Boys, jazz, Metallica.

James asked, "What's the name of the group who swears a lot?"

I said, "Guns 'n' Roses."

He said, "I've got a good arrangement for pep band of one of their songs."

Jesse said, "What song is it?"

James said, "I don't know. Name some of them."

Jesse said, "'Welcome to the Jungle.'"

James said, "No."

I said, "'Sweet Child o' Mine.'"

James said, "That's it" and pointed at me over his right shoulder.

After talking about a myriad of topics that had nothing to do with band, Jesse commented, "I remember my freshman year when Michele didn't talk much at all."

Yep, I was shy then, but I was beginning to come out of the shell I had built around me. I realized I had to start speaking up more, or I would get run over.

Our conversation managed to get back to band when Dan said something about having three helping with guard.

James said, "Yeah, and Michele and I do the rest."

Dan said something else, but I can't remember now what he did say.

Then James corrected himself, "Three for 26 (guard), one for 16 (percussion) and Michele, Todd and I do the rest."

On Monday, October 21, I left my education class early so I could come back for stadium review. Before the band lined up to go to the gym, James handed out ballots for the band awards; the kids would be voting on most of them. He told the kids to give the ballots to either Todd or me.

On the way to the gym, I walked past the single line of kids and almost ran Eric down as he came out of the auditorium. He told me I looked nice.

In the gym I stood against the wall under a basketball goal. James introduced Ken, Todd and I as his staff. He said I was a woodwind and drill instructor. Later he introduced Dan.

At one point Dan walked up to me with his hand out to shake and told me, "Michele, you look fabulous."

Gee, thanks, Dan.

I was wearing a red-striped shirt, blue blazer, faded Gap jeans, and casual shoes. I honestly didn't think I was that nicely dressed, but apparently two of my colleagues did. Gotta love compliments, don't you? Especially when you rarely received any at all. Most of the kids had come up to me with questions unlike they did the previous year. This made me only want to be a teacher even more.

At the first sectional football game, the kids were mad because they had to march. It had rained so the field wasn't all that great outside. I sat in the office until it was time to go to the field and looked at the state band finalists. Kokomo made it. Those lucky Kats!

Over at the football field, it rained on and off until halftime. I was glad I had my umbrella. Just as the fourth quarter began, it poured so James told them to go inside.

James, Larry and I sat in the office until the kids had all left.

"Are you going to state finals tomorrow?" Larry asked me.

"I don't have anyone to go with me," I said.

He asked, "Would you like to go with me?"

I didn't know what to say. I didn't really answer Larry until all three of us were leaving.

When he asked me again, I told him, "Sure." Might as well since he brought it up. Besides, I really wanted to see Kokomo since I never got to march with them at state finals.

The next day I met Larry at the McDonald's at State Road 37 and Interstate 465, and he drove us to the Dome. He parked in a garage across from the dome giving us an easy walk to see the best bands in the state.

Just as we were about to the ticket booths, Larry said, "Fancy meeting you here."

I looked to see whom he was talking to, and James and Tracey were walking toward us.

James asked, "Do you have your tickets?"

Larry said, "No."

"Go get them, and we'll wait," James told us.

We followed James since he seemed to know where he was going.

After Class A finished, Tracey asked me, "Who are you rooting for?"

I said, "Kokomo." I even told James he was rooting for Kokomo. He was wearing a blue T-shirt and a red sweater.

He said, "Red and blue are Kokomo's colors?"

I said, "Yeah."

He said, "You didn't have to redo your wardrobe when you moved down here, did you?"

I said, "Nope."

As Class A bands did a retreat, all of us stood to stretch. I looked at James, past Tracey, to hear him tell me, "We're giving Kokomo the benefit of the doubt."

On Monday, October 28, the annual band banquet was held in the cafeteria. I had lots of fun. My name, spelled correctly might I add, was in the program and listed as staff assistant.

A couple of weeks later I went to see James at school. I got all kinds of "Hi's" from the kids because I had gotten there right at the end of sixth period or symphonic band.

"Did you get my note?" I asked James.

He said he had and thanked me.

Since James was busy, I decided to leave. I got to the doorway of his office.

James stopped me and asked, "Are you going to Florida with us?"

"I don't know because I have to observe for one of my classes," I said as I moved back toward his desk. I was back to the doorway when I thought of something else.

I asked, "Will you be ordering jackets?"

He told me, "Just go to Super Sports and tell them that you want a jacket like Mr. B's."

I asked, "Do you think any of the kids would be interested?"

He told me to find out a price and he would ask. "Do you want lined or unlined?" he asked.

I told him, "I don't know. What do you recommend?"

"I wear the lined more than the unlined because we're in cold weather more," he said. "I even wear the lined in cool weather."

"I think that's probably what I'll get," I said.

James had a conference with a parent so I left.

Getting a jacket showing my love of the Marching Artesians wasn't an easy task. The following Wednesday I stopped at Super Sports to order a jacket. The woman said they didn't do the straight lettering, only the diagonal, as I tried to describe what the jacket looked like. I was so furious so I went to see James at 12:30 P.M.; the students only had a half-day. He wasn't in his office, and I couldn't get in to leave him a note so I left a note under his windshield wiper on his van.

A couple of days later, I stopped to see James about the jackets again. He was probably getting really tired of me bugging him about it, but the jacket was important to me. It set me aside from the kids since I resembled them in size and facial looks.

James told me, "Super Sports is a bunch of bull. Go by my house, get my good marching band jacket and take it with you to Super Sports." He wanted me to come up with an order form he would make copies of. "I'll even pay for your jacket," he said.

I asked him, "Is Tracey home right now?"

When James said she was, I decided to go get the jacket then. I got the jacket and went to Super Sports where I got sizes and costs. I then came up with an order form and told him I didn't set a deadline.

He said, "When do you want it?"

I told him, "I could come get it next Friday."

He said, "Okay."

As I had told him, a week later I went to see James and pick up the orders.

When he came out of the choir and orchestra office, next door to his office, he looked at me and said, "You're going to be mad at me."

I asked, "Why?"

He told me that all he had managed to do was spill coffee on the order form. I bugged him one more time before Christmas break. He told me the copy machine was broke. Okay, now I was beginning to think someone was trying to tell me something, but I wasn't about to give up that easily. I wouldn't give up without a fight.

A couple of weeks after Christmas break was over, I went to see James yet again. I asked him if he had done anything with the jacket orders. He had four kids who each wanted one and had given the rest of the kids until Monday.

"I will be able to go to Florida with the band," I said.

"I'll pay half," he said.

"When do you want the money?" I asked.

"By March 1," he said.

As I started to leave, he told me to come by, and he would help me put the order together.

"I'll be by on Friday since I don't have class or work," I said.

A week later I went to pick up the jacket orders from James. James informed Todd and me to come to his house the next Friday at 7 P.M. for a staff meeting to decide on music for the fall. I figured the more important, or maybe I should say paid, staff had already decided. I had the jacket orders so I left to go get them ordered.

A couple of weeks later Super Sports called and said the jackets were done. I picked them up, brought them home and discovered that they hadn't put the logo on the front left side. I took the jackets back.

Three days later the moment I had been waiting for finally happened. I finally got my very own staff jacket.

The next Tuesday I dropped off the jackets at school. I placed the box of jackets on a chair in the band office. I then went to find James in the band room, but he wasn't there. I returned to his office, and he was there. He had put the box on the floor.

I said, "There you are. The bill for those is in the box."

He pulled out the bill and laid it on his desk. I gave him the money for Florida, and he gave me a receipt.

Just as I got to the doorway, James said, "Did you get your jacket out?"

I said, "Yeah."

He said, "Did you get a blue one?"

I said, "Yeah." I paused and said, "Thanks."

The kids wore red ones. Why would I want a red one? Heck, I already looked like them as it was. I certainly didn't need to dress like them. I know he was probably just making sure, and I think at the end he knew how important it was to me. The whole band and being on staff was very important to me at this point. I had friends, or, at least, I considered them somewhere between acquaintance and friend in most of the staff. The kids were a great bunch of kids. I had only hoped things would continue to be good if not better than good.

♫

Chapter 10

The week before the band's trip to Florida, I stopped to see James to pick up an itinerary for the trip, and he gave me a little black booklet with all of the details of the trip south. James's student teacher, Greg, would be going.

On the Friday night before we were to leave, I felt my blood moving very rapidly through my veins. I was really excited, but I did dread the long bus ride down and back. I hoped to have tons of fun in between. I finished packing as much I could and then went to bed hoping to get some sleep. Yeah, right. Me sleep the night before I got to travel to one of my most favorite places?

On Saturday, March 21, I got up at 8 A.M. and stayed in bed for a while. I was ready to go and very excited to say the least. Mom took me to school at 11 A.M., but no one was there yet. When we came back at 11:10, a bunch of students and parents had come, but the buses weren't there yet. I went inside to see what was going on. James and Tracey were eating lunch in the band office.

Greg spoke to me, and I replied, "Hi, how are you?"

Sam Lawrence, our tour escort from Star Tours in Bloomington, came into the office. James asked him if the buses had arrived yet. Sam told him no and said they were running a little behind.

A few minutes later, I walked outside, and the buses had arrived. I went to my car, got my big white Samsonite suitcase and my olive green American Tourister carry-on, the same carry-on that made it to England and back five years before, and then proceeded to the bus to get a good seat. I took pictures of everyone loading. What a mess! Despite the fact the buses were late, we did actually leave on time at 12:30 P.M.

On the bus I sat with Greg, or rather he sat down with me. He seemed pretty nice, not to mention good-looking, but I'm sure he was probably already taken. The good ones usually were. The kids started bugging him to start a movie as soon as we got on the road, but Greg told them to wait until we got on the interstate in an hour or so.

At 2:15 P.M. we crossed the Ohio River and into Louisville, Kentucky. We stopped at a rest area so that everyone could stretch and use the restroom. That was our first stop since we had left Martinsville. When we left, it was 32 degrees and no sun. However, by then the sun came out making it a much warmer day. Within an hour or so, we stopped again, no unloading, just a switching of drivers.

At 6:30 P.M. we stopped again for supper at Morrison's Cafeteria in Nashville, Tennessee. I had my food, great food I might add, and was sitting at a small table, a table for two, when Greg asked if he could sit with me. How could I tell him no? He asked me many questions about the band, and he talked about his own high school band. We had quite a conversation, and I enjoyed every minute of it. Now why couldn't I find a nice guy like him? Our table was next to a window looking out into a mall. James, who had already eaten, walked over to the window and waved at us. He then asked if we had gotten enough to eat.

I said, "Yeah."

At 7:30 P.M. we continued our journey to Florida stopping again for a break about a half hour into Georgia a little after 10 P.M. The boys and girls had to separate so Greg ended up in the back and one of the girls was sent to me. Didn't want any hanky panky going on.

At 4:15 A.M. we stopped to switch drivers one more time. Bud, our new driver, turned out to be the best driver we had had so far. At this time we had also just crossed the state line into Florida. I finally fell asleep for three hours. When I awoke, I discovered it had rained for a little bit, but then the sun shined its pretty face.

At 8:30 A.M. we stopped at Titusville, a couple of minutes away from Kennedy Space Center, to eat breakfast at McDonald's. As they got off the buses, the kids, especially those who had never been to Florida, went crazy over the palm trees. It was so funny watching them stare and sometimes touch a tree like they had just landed on Earth from outer space.

As I stood in line for my much-awaited breakfast, a man told me I looked mature for my age. I told him I was staff. He asked me where we were from, and I told him Indiana. He then said he had lived in Florida for 10 years and was from Ohio.

At 9:30 A.M. we headed on the buses for the space center, the educational part of the trip as we were required to do by the school board. When we got there, the kids stayed on the buses, and the staff stood outside talking about the IU-LSU game, part of the NCAA tourney, while we waited on Sam to find out what we would do since we missed our tour time.

We ended up watching the 30-minute IMAX film *The Dream Is Alive*. After that was over, we ventured into the gift shop, where I bought a T-shirt, four pictures, and a mug. Might as well do something important to kill time. I loved buying souvenirs to remind me of the places I'd been.

At 11:55 A.M. we left on the guided bus tour and saw the launch pads and other stuff I had already seen on my trip with my family a few years before. After almost two hours we ended up back at the visitor's center where we were given 15 minutes to grab some lunch and get back on the buses. Some kids were late so we left 15 minutes later than planned.

Despite the fact that it was raining hard, we went to Cocoa Beach. When we arrived a few minutes later, it was still trying to rain, and the wind blew hard making the air chilly. The silly kids still went swimming. I guess it was because this was the only opportunity for them to do so, possibly the first and last time they would ever see the Atlantic Ocean. They could also go back home and brag about how they had swum in the ocean in the freezing cold. That always made you look cool if you did something crazy.

At 4:45 P.M. we left the beach for Orlando so that we could check into the Quality Inn on Lee Road, the hotel where we would stay during our brief vacation.

At 6:20 we spotted the sign on top of the hotel welcoming the band. That was cool seeing "Martinsville High School Band" in the spotlight! The kids hollered excitedly. After checking into the hotel and finding our rooms, we freshened up and got ready to leave for the Visage, a nightclub where we ate pizza, danced and socialized; it was closed to the public so we had the whole place to ourselves.

We arrived at the club at 8. Domino's brought us 70 pizzas, too many because some was left. I guess they thought we would be famished after our freezing cold swim in the ocean. Nope, they were wrong, especially when most of us didn't go swimming. After I grabbed a couple of pieces, I started to a round table.

James walked past me, pointed behind him at a table, and said, "Michele, the staff is sitting over at that table."

After eating pizza to give us some energy, the kids somehow managed to get Tracey and me out on the dance floor, and we danced a little, which the kids thought was neat.

At 10:45 after a bunch of the kids complained that they wanted to go back to the hotel, we finally left. We had lights out at midnight.

On Monday, March 23, we got a wake-up call at 6 A.M. We were almost late in my room because with four of us took longer to get ready. After eating breakfast at a place called Allie's, we left for the Magic Kingdom at Disney World. We arrived backstage at the park and got an orientation about the band's performance.

As we began touring the Magic Kingdom, I hung around James, Tracey, Sam, and Dan. We were going to ride the Pirates of the Caribbean, but it was shut down. We did the haunted house, and I shared the car with James and Tracey. We saw the pig and cow with the Mickey Mouse heads on them and the Hall of Presidents. It had been a long time since I had been to Disney World. Let me think – at least 12 years and probably more. I was only seven maybe eight years old. I didn't really remember much of what we were seeing.

At almost 1:30 P.M. James, Sam, and Dan left Tracey and me behind so they could get the band ready for their performance.

Tracey and I did some shopping until we went to the second floor of the train station to get a good seat. Eric and his wife, Eric's parents and Eric's brother were already there. Tracey introduced me to Eric's mom as a dedicated alumnus of the band.

At 2:45 the band came out of some doors on our left. They were so excited. I only wished I could have marched with them. Once the band was a good distance down Main Street, Tracey and I decided to do some more shopping. No point in standing there when there was serious shopping to be done, especially since the men weren't with us.

A little over an hour later, we met James, Sam and Greg at the backstage door. We decided to try the Pirates of the Caribbean and followed it with Thunder Mountain, my very first ride on a roller coaster. It wasn't as bad as I thought it would be. We were going to ride Space Mountain, another roller coaster, but we didn't have time to stand in line before our reservations for dinner at the castle, expensive, but great food. It was a perk from our tour director. Thanks, Sam. After we were all gathered, we rode the ferry across the lake, loaded the buses to go back to the hotel, and arrived at the hotel at 10:30 P.M. The end of a long day, a day to be remembered for a long time.

On Tuesday, March 24, my roommates decided to get up at 6 A.M., a half hour before wake-up call, since we didn't have enough time to get ready the day before.

After eating breakfast at the Holiday Inn's Comedy Club down the street, we headed to the MGM Studios for another fun-filled day. Sam was nice to have here because none of us had ever been there before. We did the Star Tours ride first, cool ride I must say, and then tried to get in to see the Indiana Jones Stunt Show, but it was already full. When we finally got into the stunt show, a senior band member volunteered as an extra. We gave her a bad time every time we saw her the rest of the day. We rode the Backlot tour ride, which was neat except you got a little wet. We ate supper at the Brown Derby, which was supposed to be one like in Hollywood, another expensive, but great food place.

At 7 P.M. we departed for the hotel and arrived about 45 minutes later. Before any of the kids got off the bus, James wanted me to hand out a Disney Magic Music Days pin to each of them. When that job was completed, I took my stuff up to my hotel room and then went to the pool outside where many of the kids were either swimming or socializing and/or both. James was handing out the Disney Magic Music Days T-shirts. I gave him the extra pins, got my shirt, and talked to Dan as he began handing the shirts out. Dan left, and I handed out the shirts. Talk about job turnover. At curfew around 9:30, I went to my room, packed my suitcase a little better and went to bed. I sure was tired.

On Wednesday, March 25, bright and early at 4:30 A.M., we were up to get loaded for our cruise that departed at 9:30 A.M. from Palm Beach. As I walked toward the third bus, our cool bus driver Bud took my white suitcase and asked me how I was.

I told him, "Fine. How are you?"

He replied, "Fine, thanks."

At 6 A.M. we left for the Port of Palm Beach with our sack of orange juice, an apple and Danish, which I never ate. I wasn't feeling very well, a sore throat, and fell asleep soon after the bus started moving down the interstate.

Because of the strong winds, the symphonic band didn't do the concert on the huge ship, reminded me of the Love Boat, only probably not near as big, as planned. I did take a motion sickness pill, but I never did get sick. I didn't think I would. Heck, I grew up around a lake and rode in speedboats. I think 75% of the band and chaperones did get sick, though. I couldn't believe how many sick kids and parents we had all over the boat. James said he would never do a cruise again. Most of the time I sat with James, Tracey and Sam on the upper deck looking out over the swimming pool. We could watch many of our kids trying to get a tan between raindrops.

At 2:30 when Sam came back from one of the lower decks, he told us the kids, parents, and staff whom we saw on this deck were the only ones who hadn't gotten sick, only about 25 out of 145 people. That was because some people psyched themselves up so much thinking they knew they would get sick that they did.

At 4 P.M. I was one of the first ones off of the boat when it docked. We left for Orlando within a half hour and ate supper at Morrison's

Cafeteria. Greg and I shared a booth next to where Brennemans and Harrises sat.

Tracey told me that those who survived the cruise are going to get T-shirts that said, "I survived the Viking Princess," (the ship's name).

When we were back on the buses, we headed for home and back to good ol' Martinsville.

On Thursday, March 26, at 12:30 A.M. just inside Georgia, we stopped so that they could switch drivers. We had to say good-bye to Bud.

He looked at me and said, "Take care."

I said, "You, too."

I slept most of the way home and caught up on all of that sleep I missed over the last few days. Boy, it's tough traveling with a band, but I loved every minute of it. I would love to go again sometime if I'm ever given the opportunity.

At 5:30 P.M., we arrived back home. Mom and Dad had brought my dark blue Sunbird to the high school so I took my stuff and put it in my car.

About a month later I went to see James and gave him some pictures of the band in Florida. He informed Greg that he put the pictures in a book.

This trip was one of the best memories about being a staff member, something I will never forget. I can't even begin to write in words what it meant to me to be able to go on something like that.

♫

Chapter 11

I knew things could only get better for me in the 1992 marching season, especially after the great previous year. In fact, I think I was still on a high from the Florida trip. I loved that trip to Florida. I mean I really loved it. I had never gotten to do anything when I was in band let alone being a staff member and getting to go. Besides, who could resist Mickey Mouse?

James had a week in June for practice like he had done the year before. I didn't really do much to help, but James did introduce me as staff. The band seemed absolutely huge to me, especially when they were all together doing fundamentals. I had my funny feeling back, like something good was going to happen to the band, like we would kick some booty. Dan had a new guy named Chase helping him that year.

After practice one Thursday night in James's office, Dan sat down next to me, put his head on my shoulder so dramatically and said, "Michele, I am so tired."

I didn't say anything; I didn't know what to say. Heck, I had a grown man putting his head on my shoulder like I was his mother.

Dan then introduced me to Chase by telling him, "Michele and I didn't talk the first year she was here, but now we have become really good friends."

I still didn't really say anything. The idea of him calling me a friend really got me, especially when we didn't really talk very much except during four months of marching band season.

A month passed by very quickly. July band practices went pretty well. James showed me how to take attendance, which was my responsibility from then on. At the end of the month, we started teaching the field show drill. This show seemed so scary because it was exciting; that year's music was from a movie called *Hook* starring one of my favorite actors Robin Williams. I really liked this music; I liked it so much that I had gone out and bought the soundtrack and then eventually the movie when it came out on video. I began praying that the band would make it to state.

For one practice James had me go to his house and pick up the state fair block, the way he had them lined up to do the state fair show that he had left on his printer. That was weird leaving practice and going to his house to get something.

The August practices, which included band camp, went pretty well. Speaking of band camp, James decided to do initiation during the day to avoid disaster. I missed that excitement since I had to work. The last practice before Band Day was spent running through the show about a dozen times.

On Wednesday, August 12, the Marching Artesians once again competed at the Indiana State Fair Band Day. After the band's morning performance, I walked with Sherri and Marci, both of whom helped Dan, to get some lunch from a concession stand.

A few minutes later Eric, James and the Youngs joined us at our table under the tent. Max Young, the former percussion instructor and now a band dad, asked about what other contests the band would compete.

James told him we might go to Kokomo "to keep Michele happy" and looked at me.

Max said, "Kokomo-Haworth?"

I said, "Yeah, my freshman year and Kokomo my sophomore year."

James broke the brief silence by asking, "And your junior year?"

I said, "Martinsville."

After we finished eating, we headed to the bleachers to watch the remaining bands compete in the morning prelims. Right before results were announced, I heard my name called out and turned to my right.

A few people down the bleachers from where I sat were looking my way, and I connected the voice to James's. He said, "I'm sorry."

I said, "For what?"

He said, "For leaving your name out of the program."

I didn't know what to say. I wondered if Tracey had said something to him, and I was right. On the way to our supper and resting time, Tracey continued to give him a bad time.

He once again said, "Hey, Michele, I'm really sorry."

I said, "Larry griped about it last year. I wasn't going to say anything." Yes, it bothered me because I probably did more than any of the rest of the alumni volunteers, but there really wasn't anything James could do now. It was over and done with. Hundreds of programs were being bought without my name in them. Oh, well.

We didn't go to Ponderosa that year like we had in previous years. Instead, we went to a city park there in Indianapolis where we had a picnic, sandwiches provided by McDonald's and the rest of the food by the kids. I just thought this was a great idea because we could eat and then rest without having to leave and ride buses.

Well, the evening performance was even better than the morning. We finally got an even numbered placing – sixth!

The practices once school started changed in the discipline approach, an idea that I told James. Kokomo's band had to do 10 push-ups whenever someone talked and/or moved during attention. James decided to have them do five since some of them would be lucky to get that many done. It seemed to work okay.

Before practice one night James told me that we were going to Kokomo for their contest. I couldn't have been happier! Back to my old stomping grounds again!

At a different practice I just happened to be wearing the right colored T-shirt. Let me explain. I walked over to the football field with James and Larry. James didn't say too much until Dan got there. Then James pointed at my shirt, my bright pink Hard Rock Café T-shirt from Orlando, one that I had bought when I went with my parents to Florida at the end of June and first of July, and made a comment about how bright it was. He then told Dan that he should use that color as the last flag.

James went into a long spiel about how he related the pink to the song the band played and then once again pointed at my shirt, "That's why that color would be neat."

One Tuesday practice after music sectionals, James told Larry and me that he wouldn't give the kids much time to adjust. Larry and I were to find a couple of key people and set them in their right spots and then let everyone else adjust themselves. I couldn't believe how much the kids really wanted me to help, raising their hands, yelling my name. I felt extremely happy, though.

On Saturday, September 19, Plainfield High School was the site of our first "real" contest of the 1992 season, and the band really kicked some tail. The practice before we left seemed great. James's lecture about self-discipline, work ethic and confidence at an earlier practice still seemed to have some effect on them. Anyway, I worked my tail off those two and a half hours fixing forms. I still didn't know what to expect our first contest. They had a great show, the best I think we had ever seen.

I was the only one who rode with Brennemans to the contest. The band looked good considering it was the first contest. Their score of 61.4 points gave them a third place finish. I may have been right; state finals could have been in the works. Wouldn't that have been great? On the way home I kept thinking about how much fun I had had that day. I loved being around this band, especially since I felt very comfortable with the kids.

The following Saturday it rained from 7 to 11 A.M. so James had the band practicing music inside, which they needed to do anyway. James wasn't sure that the band would go to Kokomo, and all I knew was that I would be really disappointed.

Well, Kokomo was on; they hadn't had much rain, according to someone James spoke to on the phone. Oh, good, was all I could think. We left a little late, but at least we went. We stopped at Carmel so James could call to see if the contest was still on; it had been raining. The bands were performing in the auditorium. However, by the time we got there, they were marching on the soggy field. The kids marched an okay show scoring 59.4 and placing third, only three-tenths behind Lafayette Jefferson High School, usually a tough competitor.

After we performed as we walked back to the buses, Mrs. Scholl, a former Kokomo band parent when I lived there, I think I have mentioned her before, caught up to me, and I got a hug. I was so surprised to see her because her youngest child was my age; she didn't even need to be there.

We left as soon as the kids changed out of their uniforms and put their instruments away. Eric stayed with the drum majors for results. James decided on McDonald's for supper for those riding with him.

As soon as we finished eating, we headed for Greenwood for the second contest of the day. During the entire contest, it drizzled rain except during awards. We received a third place finish and tied Concord (Remember them from state fair?) for best percussion.

In critique, which is when the band directors spoke to the judges about their show and scores, Tracey and I went with the directors. The food, provided by the hosting band, was great, and being able to talk to the judges was interesting. One judge didn't understand the pink flag. Well, we were doing the music from *Hook*, as I've already mentioned. In the movie it shows the little girl singing once she's been kidnapped by Captain Hook. The band played that music as part of the closing song so the flag was pink. Make sense? At least that's the way I interpreted what it meant, and I'm pretty sure that's the way it was supposed to be. That one judge became a big joke to us for the next week or so. How could you not understand? Another judge said he loved our show and would be at district the next week. I sure hoped he remembered us and remembered what he had told us. It was always helpful when a judge liked you because you would get the higher score.

On Saturday, October 3, I woke up at 9:45 A.M. and grabbed lunch at Burger King before practice started at 11 A.M. During practice I walked out to fix a saxophone line, and James noticed and asked me to fix it. Yes, James, I know. The kids didn't really seem to be fired up, but I figured they would be. Deborah, a clarinet player, became sick during practice.

At the ISSMA District contest during warm-ups, as I walked around checking uniforms, Deborah didn't look okay so I asked her. She said she was. Two minutes later she called me over and asked if she could go sit down.

Before they went to perform, I asked her if she would be okay. She said, "Yeah."

I told her I would be there on the track if she felt sick.

I couldn't stand waiting for the results; the band looked so great. You know that's the thing about practice. You could have the worst one in the world, but when it came to competition, the kids would perform their hearts out. It was like they were saving all of their strength for what mattered.

Well, we obtained a Division I trophy and a score of 66.75 beating Southport! Woohoo! I told Sherri that I hoped we beat them, and we did.

Once we were back at the high school, I stood with my back to the door that led into the music suite.

Deborah put her arm around me and said, "Thank you."

I was so surprised that I didn't know what to say. I knew right then that I had made the right decision to become a teacher. I cared about what happened to the kids.

The next week's practices were pretty decent. Bill Robertson, our music composer, was there to work with the band for one and a half hours. Once we got them to the field, the band sounded so good. Dan, Larry and I watched the tape from Saturday. I can't believe how good they looked. Larry thought they could be third or fourth. I was just hoping for fifth. I really envied this band because I wish I was marching this show. Later, after we got scores from the other district sites, we decided we could be at least seventh at regional. I really thought we could have a shot at top five if the kids each gave 110%.

The weekend of October 10 and 11 was a busy one for the Marching Arties. We had a contest at Center Grove High School and the Fall Foliage Festival parade.

As soon as we got the kids on the bus for the contest at CGHS, the rain came down. By the time we arrived at the school, the rain stopped. The contest was in the gym even though it wasn't raining, just lightning. If it wasn't for the fact that we were already there, James was ready to leave. We didn't perform until 10:15 P.M., one and a half hours late. I thought the band performed okay, but tempos were too fast, though.

After the band finished and headed back to the buses, Jeri, a trumpet player, passed out right outside the door. Mary, a nurse and Ken's wife, and two men got Jeri awake and up again.

After we found out Jeri would be okay, Eric asked me, "Did James say anything to you about judging tomorrow?"

I said, "No."

The band ended up placing second behind Northview High School, a state finalist.

On the way home James told me to be at the high school by 12:30 P.M. tomorrow. When I got home, my inspirational feelings wanted to come out so I wrote a letter to the editor.

On Sunday I got the opportunity once again to judge marching in the FFF parade along with Ken and Dan. Mary came with Ken, and they bought lunch at a Chinese food vendor. Mary gave me a fortune cookie, which said, "Nothing is certain but the unforeseen." I immediately thought of the band and their most important contest next week. Hmmmm??? Was something really great going to happen? Would we seriously be marching in the Dome for state finals?

The following week's practices would be the last ones if the band didn't make state finals. I couldn't bear the thought of that happening because I would definitely miss this. I rewrote my inspiring words before I gave them to Sherri at Tuesday's practice, which didn't go very well. Sherri liked what I had written and took five of my pictures to put in *The Martinsville Reporter*, trying to get the kids hyped about Saturday. I began to believe we would go to state. Sherri told me she'd been having dreams.

On Thursday Sherri told me two of my pictures ended up on the front page of the paper. I hadn't been home to see it. The practice itself was a good one, and the band looked great on the last run through. I couldn't wait to see what would happen on Saturday. My letter was in Friday night's paper. I had several kids, Tracey, and a band mom tell me they liked it at the football game. I really didn't think it was that good, but maybe it was better than I thought.

On Saturday, October 17, before practice started on the most important day of marching season, Lucy, drum major, started reading a letter that was printed in *The Martinsville Reporter* to the band with the exception of the percussion and guard.

Marty, a new staff member, asked me if Ken had written it, and I said I had. I couldn't believe that Lucy read the letter to them, but I believed it helped with practice. This was the best practice all season. I had more kids tell me how good my letter was and how inspirational it was.

At 4:30 P.M. we left for Bedford for the ISSMA Regional. We didn't say much on the way down. It was almost as though we were concentrating just as much as the kids hopefully were. When we got to the school, a Bedford North Lawrence band parent wished us good luck and then said they were going to beat us. I hoped we beat them. How rude! I was really nervous and so was the rest of the staff, especially James. Before she got into her uniform, Lilly, the student I had had the disagreement with a couple of years before, hugged me. In warm-ups she looked tense. I thought about going over to say something to her but didn't. We performed after New Castle.

Despite the cold the kids still performed an awesome show. In fact, I got goose bumps. I could only imagine what I would have been feeling had I been one of the kids. Katie, a sophomore flute player, told me she thought it was my letter that did it. Eric, James, Larry and I ended up standing outside of the gate because it was very crowded as we waited for the results. We talked as we waited. A Division I for us! However, we didn't make it to state. Darn. Eric and James went to get results while we waited to find out scores. What seemed like forever was actually just a few minutes.

Finally, the two men returned followed by Tracey, Sherri, Marci, Dan and Marty. We got sixth! We scored a 78.40, our best show since

1987! We were all so excited. We wanted to find that BNL woman to tell her that we beat them; they had a 70.3. When we got back to the buses, James got the kids off of them and told them how well they had done. They were very happy to say the least.

On the way home, Eric told me, "Michele, I hope the kids read your letter."

I said, "Lucy read it to everyone except the percussion and color guard before practice."

Over the next few days all I could think about was the band. I was so proud of them. Gees, how I wished I could have marched this show.

Stadium review was the Monday after regional. In the gym James introduced his staff halfway through the high school band's show. I was standing between Lee, the other drum major, and Lucy so that is how I got introduced. I did raise my hand, though, so the crowd could pick me out. When it was over, Dan, Billy and Jay, the two percussion instructors, Rod, James and I sat in the office for an hour discussing and listening to what we can do next year.

Like the previous year, I met Larry at I-465 and SR 37 interchange, and we went to see state finals. We got into the Dome and found seats just as the D bands started. ISSMA changed the order of the bands that year—B, C, D, A. Our seats were close to the 50-yard line. I wasn't sure about the different order, but we did get to see Monrovia, another county school, who looked great. They ended up getting fifth.

During the break between D and A bands, Larry and I stood up to stretch. We had our band jackets on. After we sat back down, I got a funny feeling that someone was looking at me and turned to my left to look. James followed closely behind by Tracey sat down next to us.

James said, "Hey, guys, what took you so long?"

They had just gotten there and had been sitting up higher. We all slid over to be on the aisle. Homestead High School from the Fort Wayne area won Class A. At least it was a different band for once. I got so sick and tired of the same one or two bands winning every year.

The last event for the 1992 Marching Artesians was on Monday, October 26, the band banquet. When I got there, I learned the staff no longer sat across the front. The band council did. The senior class gave James a ship in a bottle, which was really neat.

I was amazed by the way the kids seemed to like me. On a day when I stopped to talk to James about something, a sophomore clarinet player stopped in the doorway of Frank's office. She asked me how I was and if I was ready for marching band season. I said I was, but that I wasn't sure if I would be able to help next year. She said it wouldn't be the same without me and that I just had to help. She was practically begging me! This girl was one that had hardly spoken to me in the two years she had been in band. I must have made more of an impression than I thought I had.

During the first three months of 1993, I did my student teaching at West Middle School, the same school where Tracey taught. I know this really doesn't have anything to do with me being on staff, but it will show a relationship to what I was about to learn.

A couple of weeks into my experience, I kept waking up during one night: 1:30 A.M., 4:30 A.M., 5:30 A.M. I figured it was my nerves, but I had a dream about the band as though something had happened.

When I got to school on Tuesday, January 26, Tracey caught me in the office and asked, "Did you hear what happened to Arthur Hackett last night?"

I said, "No."

She said, "He died."

All I could say was, "Oh." Instantly, I felt almost like I was reliving Grandpa's death from about five years before all over again except this time it was happening to someone else. Tracey said something about letting me go in with James and her for flowers, but she doesn't know much about when the funeral would happen.

On Wednesday, Tracey told me the funeral was Friday and visiting hours were Thursday. Liz, Arthur's wife, had called Ken at 3 A.M. right after Arthur died. In turn Ken had called Brennemans. The pit crew dads were the pallbearers. I thought that was nice. The pit crew dads were the dads who took care of all the sideline percussion equipment like the xylophones, keyboards, tympani, and other assorted stuff. Arthur had been one of them. It sure was too bad to lose him; he was a great guy. Arthur was only 48 years old, not much younger than my own dad. The paper had a nice obituary and listed memorial contributions to either the band or Special Olympics. I decided to donate money to the band. The money was to be used to buy a much-needed trailer to haul instruments and equipment.

At 1:40 P.M. on Friday, James picked Tracey and me up in front of West for Arthur's funeral. I figured it was the least I could do for my band family. The funeral home was packed full of band kids and parents mostly. It was an amazing turnout.

During the last week of my student teaching, my supervising teacher and I went to the teacher's lounge to talk about my progress at 2 P.M. during the prep period. One of the secretaries found me and said I had a phone call.

Thinking it would be a parent, I answered the phone by saying, "This is Miss Mathews."

The voice on the other end said, "Hi, Miss Mathews, this is Mr. Brenneman." He asked me if I would come over after school and help judge drum majors.

I told him I would be there. That really surprised me that James would call and ask me to judge something like that. I realized when I got to the high school that Eric's son was trying out so James didn't want Eric as a judge. Candace became our newest drum major for the next year.

♫

Chapter 12

Well, after a great 1992 marching season, I thought the 1993 season could only get better. It did to some degree, but the disappointments were a little worse than the previous year. We still practiced the first week in June with a few weeks off before practices really got going in July. I missed the first week of practices in July because I went to Myrtle Beach with Mom and Dad. That was a hard decision for me because I love both things equally, but I did want to go on vacation, the beach is the best, so it won. I didn't figure I would miss much that first week, but it sure felt weird when I did return. I didn't know whether it was just me or what, but I didn't feel like I would do as much to help as I had the last couple of years.

The Wednesday the band marched over to the 4-H Fair for their performance, the kids weren't behaving like James thought they should have been. He made them sit down on the parking lot when we got back to the high school and gave them a lecture about self-discipline. I believed James thought this band had a chance of going to state so he was going to work them hard.

The two days before Band Day were busy ones for the band and even for me. One night at practice a reporter from *The Martinsville Reporter* came to take pictures so they would have a color picture on the front page if the band did well. I had worn my brightly colored Mickey shirt and matching cut-off denim shorts. I received many compliments on the outfit. Needless to say, James picked me as one of the people to be a part of the picture. The kids looked pretty decent during practice.

On Tuesday before the big day the band performed at the Red and Blue game. They didn't look too bad from what I could see on the ground, especially since it was raining off and on.

On Wednesday, August 11, the band traveled to the Indiana State Fairgrounds for Band Day. I rode with James, Eric, Todd, Ken and Mary. We arrived at 9 A.M. only to find out we were on an hour delay. The track was muddy. Indianapolis had had an inch of rain the night before. The one-hour delay went to a three-hour delay because the track wasn't drying like the officials wanted despite the fact it was so hot. Sherri, Marci, Chase, Dan and I walked around the fairgrounds, grabbed some lunch, and talked.

After a couple of hours, we went back to the buses and sweated with the kids. The band finally got to perform at 3:30 P.M. The heat really got to me. I didn't know if I would be okay or not. I felt a couple of times like I was going to pass out even though I had eaten and drank plenty. Wouldn't that have been funny, a staff member passing out from the heat?

After the kids performed one heck of a show, one of the guard girls squatted down and didn't look very well. I grabbed her arm gently and took her to the first aid tent. Later I got a hug from her thanking me for taking her to the tent. No problem.

We were fourth in the morning, evening "A" as James called it, and we would perform ninth in the evening.

After a long rest and supper at the park, we returned to the fairgrounds at 8 P.M. I changed my clothes to the black long-sleeved band shirt and my coral-colored shorts. Why a long-sleeved shirt you ask? Well, the kids performed music from Danny Elfman; *Music from a Darkened Theater* was the name of the show. For the Sweet 16 the kids looked better than they did the first time.

After the performance James talked to the kids telling them that he thought they looked even better than the first time and he didn't think it was possible. He then really fired them up by saying something about the Hoosier Dome. We ended up fourth. The kids were happy to say the least. I waited on Lee and Candace, the drum majors, since none of the other staff was around so that we could get our picture taken.

Lee came off of the stage and said, "Where to, Michele?"

We got lucky. A state trooper from Morgan County where Martinsville was the county seat pulled up in a golf cart and told us he would take us to the building. We arrived back at the high school at almost 2 A.M. I was really tired to say the least; the heat sure could take a lot out of you, especially when you had been out in it all day.

Remember how the saying goes, everybody is famous for 15 minutes? Well, I was famous on Thursday. The picture that the reporter had taken was on the front page. I looked a little goofy. Larry and James were shaking hands with Lee and Candace looking at all of us. I had a lot of people tell me they saw my picture in the paper. It felt kind of weird because I have never had my picture in the paper like that before.

The practices before the first contest were decent for the most part. When we discussed where to go for that first contest, James mentioned ISU at Terre Haute. Jay, Ken and Marty all wanted to go there, but I turned up my nose.

Two practices later, with Dan present James made a comment about "Michele wants to go to Lawrence Central."

I don't know why I wanted to go there, but I just thought we had a better chance of winning than at ISU. Just call it my funny feeling telling me something good was going to happen and the band had to be there.

At the first home football game the reporter came up to me and asked, "How did you like the picture on the front page?"

I told her it was nice or something like that.

She said, "Your shirt really made the picture stand out." A compliment, I guessed.

Helping the band and being a substitute teacher put me in an awkward situation so I asked James about it at practice one night. I told James that Lee called me by my first name in the hallway with several other kids standing there.

I told James, "I don't care if they call me Michele here, but when I am in this school as a substitute teacher, they need to call me Miss Mathews."

James said, "Do you want me to talk to them or do you want to?"

I said, "I don't care."

He said, "Okay, I will." He paused for a minute and then said, "I think you're at a point in your life where they need to call you Miss Mathews here, too."

At the end of that week, James still hadn't said anything to the kids. He came up to me at the game after halftime and said, "I forgot to make that announcement."

I said, "That's okay. I just want you to do it sometime soon. Kelly called me Michele in front of some other kids today when I subbed."

He said he understood what I was going through because he taught Sunday School and had kids call him James at school.

On Saturday, September 18, the band competed at the Lawrence Central Invitational. Before we left, James had a four-hour rehearsal. I enjoyed practices like this one because I helped the saxes and flutes who had absolutely no idea as to what they should be doing, which meant I got to keep busy helping them figure it out.

Well, all I can say was the practice must have paid off. We won the contest! The band also received best percussion and best music. I couldn't believe we actually won the contest beating two bands, Lake Central and Fort Wayne Northside, both of whom went to state last year. See I told you we needed to go to this contest, didn't I, James? James was so happy. I had never seen him like this before. As the band and staff walked back to the buses, James was walking in front of me, and he kept making hand motions as though he were on cloud nine.

The following week all I could think about was the band and how much I wanted to see them make state. Ken tried to get me paid, but James told me maybe next year. I didn't really care; I would be here whether I got paid or not. I loved this band, and I would do whatever it took to see that they were successful. What would I have done if I didn't have the band? I would have probably gone crazy sitting in my boring bedroom at home.

On Saturday, September 25, James ran through a couple of things the band needed to do before it started raining. At 10 A.M, he sent the kids home. He had called Columbus East where our contest for that day was to be, and someone told him the bands were standing in the gym to play. James told them we weren't coming since we were the only ones in our class. The kids returned at 2:30 for an inside practice before supper at 6.

On the way to the Greenwood contest that evening, James asked me, "How many years did you have me as band director, Michele?"

I told him two. I'm not sure why he asked me that, but I'm sure there was a reason. He never did tell me why he asked me that, and I didn't ask.

For the next few minutes on our drive, James, Ken, Craig, an alumnus and now percussion instructor, and I figured out what the band played every year since James became band director at Martinsville. The kids stood in the gym and played. They were fourth and received a participation award and best percussion.

Well, James finally remembered to talk to the kids about how to address me a week and a half after our initial chat. Better late than never as they say. I was sure James had more important things on his mind at the time, though. I ended up subbing for a half day for James.

As I headed for the band office, I passed James headed the other way. He corrected himself when he called me Michele.

"That's okay because a couple of the kids called me Michele in the hallways that day," I said.

"I'm going to yell at them," he said.

Before he left for his meeting when fifth period started, James wrote, "The name is Miss Mathews," on the board and then gave the kids a speech about calling me that whenever they see me in the hallways.

"Michele doesn't care if you call her Michele at band practice, but it would be better if you got into the habit of calling her Miss Mathews all the time," he said.

At the beginning of sixth period, which was symphonic band, I stood up in front of them and told them basically what James had told the other class. I can't believe I did that; I talked in front of around 75 kids. I was making progress but believe me it wasn't easy getting 75 kids quiet enough so they could hear me.

On Saturday, October 2, the band had another eventful day. We had a good rehearsal before we left for ISSMA District at Columbus East. Because there was a bunch of people in the band office, I didn't hear James ask me how I thought the band was going to do. Once James, Tracey and I were in the van, he asked me the question again.

"I think we could hit a 70 if they are really concentrating like last year at regional," I replied.

The band didn't do as well as we hoped. They got a 66.4 and best music with Columbus North beating us. Still not too shabby, though. James talked to the kids on each of the buses before we left. We got back to the high school at 8:30 P.M.

During practice the following week, I wore my old Kokomo clarinet sweatshirt. There was a reason for this. Let me explain. Harold Gallant, our drill writer once again, came to observe and gave us pointers. He kept looking at me funny, and James didn't introduce me to him. Actually, I figured Harold would remember me from last year. Back at the band office, Harold's curiosity couldn't take it anymore because he finally asked me if I had marched at Kokomo. Always such a small world when you know people like this.

Before our next contest on October 9, we nearly froze to death for the two and a half hours of practice. In fact, it was so cold that James let them go inside for a little bit to get warm. He had me working with the saxes and at one point asked me to fix some intervals in the low brass. I even got a "Thanks" out of him. We arrived at Center Grove High School early so James made the kids stay on the buses.

Despite the cold, I thought the kids performed very well. They got fourth place and no caption awards. It seemed like we were slipping away from any possibility of going to state as always. How could that happen?

On the way home James, Craig and I talked about the judges. James was just totally bummed out. I was, too. I just don't understand how the judges can say we are good and that they love our show and then they score us below Center Grove or whoever the best bands were. It just doesn't make any sense.

Before practice on Tuesday, I thought about calling James at school and see if he would let me give a pep talk to the band. I really thought I could do it since I had done it in class that day I subbed, but I chickened out. I decided to write my annual letter instead.

We had a good practice on Thursday. If it did rain on Saturday, they use marching scores from district and then music and general effect scores from a stand still in the gym at regional. We were currently sixth in marching with Southport and Columbus North beating us, meaning that two of the big bands were lower than us! My thoughts turned to the way we did last year. We were sixth at Band Day and sixth at regional. This year we were fourth at Band Day and hopefully fourth at regional. I just had an eerie feeling. I decided to wear my brown boots on Saturday. We won at Lawrence Central when I was wearing them so maybe they were our good luck. We found out later we were wrong about what scores they use, marching and general effect from district. We were still sixth. Basically, we had to be able to march the show, or we were done.

I dropped off my letter on the way to school the Thursday before regional. The practices were good that week before the big contest. I couldn't believe how well they were practicing. It was as though we had another band. The only thing I could figure out was that they realized how badly they really wanted to go to state.

On Saturday, October 16, I arrived at the high school a little earlier that what I had planned. A band mom came into James's office. She told me she liked my letter, which was good, and James agreed with her. That was the first time in a couple of years that he had said anything to me about the letters I had written. The practice before we left was a good one; the kids didn't really say too much, which made the practice even better.

On the long trip to Evansville, we stopped at the Executive Inn in Vincennes for a rest break, where it was sunny and warm. The rain sprinkled on us just was we entered Evansville, but it never really rained. I was glad of that. Rain sure could dampen things for a band contest.

As the band walked to warm-ups, they were very quiet, the quietest I had heard them all season. Maggie and Katie, both flute players, came up to me just before the band got ready to warm up.

"Michele, I read your letter, and I cried at the end," Maggie told me.

"Katie, did you read my letter?" I asked.

She said, "No."

"Do you remember last year at regional when you were marching off of the field and you said, 'Michele, I think your letter inspired us?'" I said.

Maggie had figured out whom I was talking about. Katie's eyes got watery. She knew then, too. I think I got her. I received a hug from both of them and then I wished them good luck. I couldn't believe the performance the band gave the crowd. They were totally awesome. Dan jumped around acting like a crazed lunatic. You should have seen him. I even got a hug from him before the kids had barely marched off the field.

Later, Damon, Maggie's dad, asked me, "Did Dan finally come off of his high?"

I said, "I think so."

Sherri, Marci and I walked over to listen to results with the directors. Well, we didn't make it to finals, and we were really bummed out when we found out we were eighth. These kids marched a better show this year than last year's. We couldn't believe it.

James gathered everyone behind the equipment truck and gave a talk. He told the kids it was a game of politics. He also said the band was a second family to him. I was standing next to Tracey. She had tears in her eyes, and I put my arm around her. This was so darn frustrating, so darn unfair. These kids deserved to march in the Dome this year.

On the way home James wanted one of us to figure out where we placed with each judge so I did it. Using the tally sheets with all of the scores for each caption and with all the bands listed, I figured out we were sixth with one music judge and 13th with the other. What??? What was that music judge listening to? Obviously, not us. The rest of the way home I just kept thinking about the awesome show the kids performed, wondering what James would do next year. I hoped he wouldn't go through what he said he would and only do state fair.

At the first sectional football game, Rod and I talked to James, or rather listened to him. It was obvious he had been thinking this about this for a while. He told us his three options for the school board: (1) get James an assistant director at the high school like he wanted, (2) don't do ISSMA, and (3) ask for James's resignation. Number 3 was a surprise for me, and I hoped he didn't really mean it.

On Tuesday, October 26, I arrived early to the band banquet. I started to sit at the front table, but James decided the staff should sit somewhere else so we put some odd-shaped tables together. Brennemans and Harrises sat together, and the rest of the staff, including Sherri, Jay, Billy, Rod, Dan, Larry, and I, all sat at the other table. James told the audience as he thanked his staff that his woodwind instructors—that would be Larry and me—apparently were writers as well since both had written letters for the newspaper. I didn't get anything but a big thanks from James.

A couple of weeks later we had a staff meeting at Brennemans' house. James told us about the superintendent backing his decision to not do ISSMA. Jay wasn't happy about that at all because he was planning on working with Martinsville only next year. He had worked with another band this past year. I wasn't happy either, but it was James's decision. His life and his family's lives had suffered enough. The superintendent didn't want to give James an assistant. We would still do state fair, but the fall would be boring.

On January 7, 1994, after the annual alumni pep band gathering, James told Rod in front of me the parent meeting would be the next Wednesday at 6:30 P.M. James had told me the previous Wednesday that the meeting would be on Monday. He didn't get a letter out to the kids like he hoped.

At the band parent meeting on Wednesday I really felt sorry for James because many of the parents didn't seem to be supporting him. They only wanted option #1 and couldn't even think about option #2. I wanted option #1 just as much as they did, but they didn't realize how much time James spent at school through marching band season. He deserved help from an assistant. As much as I really hated to see ISSMA end because we were on a roll, James couldn't continue like he was. I was a little nervous about what would happen.

Early in March I borrowed a brochure James had gotten from the Carmel band and worked on one to recruit eighth graders for our band. When I got a sample put together, I decided to go see James, but the van wasn't there so I didn't stop. When I got home after a trip to the library, the answering machine had a message from James at 2:09 P.M.

He said, "Michele, this is James Brenneman. I can't remember whether I told you or not, but we're having a staff meeting on Sunday at 6:30. We'd love to have you. Thanks. Bye."

Two days later at the staff meeting Bill Robertson, our music arranger, came so we could talk about the band's music for next year.

At the school board meeting in mid May, James found out they still didn't want him to have an assistant. They just wanted to put George York, the director at West Middle, and Eric, who taught at East Middle, at the high school for part of the day to lessen James's load.

At the music department awards banquet on May 31, James told Dan and me, "Since I will have George and Eric at the high school one period a day, I'm going to do ISSMA." That was what the school board was telling him.

"I'm looking for a job elsewhere," James also told us.

I wasn't sure whether he was just making a comment or he meant what he said. I didn't ask. He was scaring me because I didn't want him to leave here, and I could tell Dan didn't either.

On the last day of school, I stopped to see James in the early afternoon. The man from Paige's Music Store in Indianapolis was there and talked about Edgewood High School and other band director openings and scared me in the process. He left, and I asked James if he was looking for a job.

He answered, "Not seriously."

This whole situation was really scaring me. I wanted James to stay. He had built the band program up so much in the years that I had been associated with it. I hated to see him leave and have someone else destroy everything he had worked hard to do. That wouldn't be fair to the kids at all, but, on the other hand, I knew James had to do what he felt was right and make himself happy. I would support him in any way I could; it was the least I could do after he had allowed me to help this wonderful band.

♫

Chapter 13

Well, the 1994 marching season started out better than I thought it would. I discovered I got a job at *The Martinsville Reporter* the same day that the week of June practices started on June 6. At least I would have a job for the summer. Heck, who knows? Maybe I would be writing about the band, which I thought would be really nice to have someone finally cover them like they should be. At the practices I helped Eric with the new members. That was fun. I was making my first impression on a bunch of kids who didn't know me. Not that I was out to make friends, but at least with someone nice like me, why would they want to quit?

A couple of weeks later I had a dream about James's kids telling me they were moving to Kansas. This dream scared me because I didn't want them to move that far away. Their friendship meant a lot to me. I didn't know what I would do if James left here. I guess it depended on if he really got another job and on whom his replacement was here. I don't know if I could continue working with the band without James, but the rest would probably stay providing the new director didn't fire them.

At the first practice in July, I found out James was up for a job at Edgewood. If he got it, he would be gone. I didn't look for him to be around here much longer. He said he would continue looking for another job because he disliked this place and was bitter about what the school board did to him. He still wasn't getting what he truly wanted, a full-time assistant like all other Class A bands had. Dan was scared and wondered what was going to happen.

When practices resumed in July, the band looked really good, and we got some good news. Eric got the East Middle School assistant principal job, and James decided to stay, saying he didn't want to leave us high 'n' dry. He decided to see if the school board would hire a music department secretary. Eric suggested me for the job, and James agreed because he wouldn't have to teach me much.

Band camp was okay, but I didn't get to do much since I was working in the morning and early afternoon. I did enjoy the moments when I was there, though, as always. I mean working with the band was always fun, wasn't it?

On Friday James had me acting like his secretary. I took his deposit to the bank and called to find out prices on new staff jackets.

With about a week to go before Band Day I decided I didn't know how the band would do. They didn't seem to be working very hard, and I didn't see the determination that I had seen the last couple of years.

On Wednesday, August 10, I was up at 5:45 A.M., and the band and its caravan left the high school at 7:30. I rode in Brennemans' van along with Eric, George, Rod, Jay, and Camden, a new percussion instructor. I ate lunch with Sherri and Marci, and the three directors joined us.

After obtaining results we went to the park for a few hours of rest and supper. We had our pep talk with James and couple of students. James told the kids he was glad he didn't leave. The kids sure were pumped for the night show. They marched better at night for whatever reason. The band was awesome but still got fourth with best percussion. The second, third, and fourth places had only a one or two point spread.

At the buses James told the kids, "This is only the beginning."

I sure hoped he was right. These kids deserved to march in the Dome on October 22.

James wanted me to order new staff jackets. I stopped to talk to him about them a week after our big day.

"Michele, as far as I'm concerned, you're my new secretary, but the higher officials have to ask the riffed ones first," he said.

That meant I probably wouldn't get the job. It would have been nice to be able to do the secretary thing in the afternoon to give me the feeling of a full-time job.

Do you know how practices never seemed that great once we went to Band Day? I mean the kids just seemed to not care once we did Band Day, but this particular year, the practices seemed to be better than ever. The kids were quiet and worked hard. Maybe it bothered them that James could have left. I don't know. However, I had never seen a show look this good this early before. James said we would be in the Dome, and I agreed.

On Saturday, September 17, I went over for the 2 P.M. practice, which went well. The kids seemed to be really getting into this. We went back to Lawrence Central High School to defend our title. Remember we won the year before so it was a must we participate that year. I hoped they would make it to state. James over-estimated the time so Joe, a new color guard instructor who replaced Chase, taught the arm movements for the start of the show. He didn't get done, but what he taught looked neat. Well, the band didn't look too bad; they won best percussion and third place. The score was not too bad, and James seemed happy.

The following Saturday right before practice started, James called Ben Davis to see if they were still having the contest outside, and A and B bands would be. We had had rain during the night, and it was muddy. We had a decent rehearsal. The kids sure were working hard this year. Ben Davis officials lied to us or else changed their minds after James called. No one marched outside. A and B bands stood in the gym and played; the field was muddy and water stood in the pit area, the area along the front sideline. The kids played very well standing still, or at least James said they did. They still got best percussion and drum major and third place. We went back to the high school for a supper break.

At Greenwood the kids did great. Not only were they Class A champion and won awards for best percussion, best music and best auxiliary, but they won grand champion! They beat Lawrence North by one-tenth of a point, just like James told them they would. I couldn't believe that. You have to know that Lawrence North is a band that has gone to state for many years. Heck, they even made state when I was in band years before, and here we were beating them. It wasn't by much at all, but at least it was something. The kids ran up to the buses. James had gone to the hospital with a student so he didn't hear the results or go to the critique. He was pleased. Tracey hadn't gone to the contest, but she wished she had. The one time we won a contest, and she didn't go.

On Saturday, October 1, the big day, whether the band went onto regional the next week, ISSMA District. I went to practice at 10:30 A.M. carrying a box of new staff jackets. It sure seemed like a nice day until several kids got sick. I took one girl to the band room in my car. It was really hot, hotter than what we realized. James was up in the press box and had no idea how hot it was since he was in the shade. He said he wished someone had said something. He evidently didn't pay any attention to us carrying kids off the field left and right just like in a bloody battle scene.

On the way to Columbus East, James told me he was pleased with the jackets, white satin with blue lettering. I was certainly glad of that. Well, we got a Division I along with best music and placed second behind Columbus North.

The one really good thing about being a reporter for the local paper was that I got do the band stuff as I had hoped I would. The band parents were eating that up. No one had ever covered the band like I was doing even though the paper said they would accept whatever we wanted to put in the paper. For instance, I put together the band insert, or yearbook, whatever you would prefer to call it, which came out on Friday, October 7. I got a lot of compliments as I did for most of the work, including the photos and articles.

On Saturday, October 8, at our do-or-die contest, or regional, the kids had an okay practice. It seemed almost like they burned out and didn't even want to be there. However, sometimes when they have an okay practice, they do better at the contest. We had a short trip to Bedford. I was a little nervous as the band warmed up. I felt like they were going to do really well even if they didn't make it to state. They performed very well considering how tough the show was; they were playing music from *On the Waterfront*. I was pleased and so was most of the staff. The kids even knew they had done well, and they were usually the ones who told the staff.

As we waited for results several hours later, my new man Liam (Yes, I was dating and engaged!) and I watched the other bands. We managed to catch up with James, Tracey, and Dan as the results were called out. The band got a Division I but no state final placing, which we didn't think would happen anyway. Tracey, Liam and I waited as Dan and James went to get the envelope with the judges' tapes and results. James looked really disappointed as he, followed by Dan, Jay, Camden, and Darrell Evans, our new assistant director, came from the bleachers. James told us we wouldn't believe where we placed. We were 13th. What in the hell were those judges looking at? Excuse my French, but that is absolutely ridiculous. James told the kids when we got back to the buses, and instantly some of them were in tears. Candace went to pieces, and Lee comforted her. I felt so sorry for the kids. They had worked so hard. By the time we got to Brennemans' van, parked with the other cars, it was raining pretty hard. James was so mad he didn't know what to say.

On the following day I had to judge the bands for FFF parade. Liam and I went to the high school to catch our ride downtown. As we waited in James's office, the kids kept coming to his door and looking at James like he was going to say the whole thing was a mistake. However, he couldn't give them any answers because he didn't understand himself. I couldn't believe how devastated the kids were. Some of them didn't even want to march in the parade.

On Monday after I finished work, I ventured to see James and give him pictures of the band from district. He received a secretary, but it wasn't me.

On Tuesday at practice I asked Candace how she was doing after Saturday. She said fine and she couldn't wait until winter drumline. I think practice was a waste of time. The kids didn't really care anymore, and I didn't do much to help. It was really too cold to do anything. James started talking about how we would do next year's show. Simplify everything were the two key words.

On Saturday, October 15, the band attended its last contest at Carmel High School. I think the kids and staff wished we didn't have to do it, especially after our disappointing weekend the week before. In fact, they didn't do much better. They placed sixth out of six bands in our class. Liam and I were sitting behind our band in the bleachers when some of them got up and started yelling, "We got screwed," over and over again. I told James about it on the way home, and he said he would take care of it on Monday. Even though that was what happened, the kids shouldn't have behaved that way; they should have kept their opinions to within our group. Yes, they were right, but yelling it for everyone to hear wasn't appropriate. Sorry, guys, but you shouldn't have done that; you were still representing Martinsville. I can't help it the judges are blind.

As we always did, the band's marching season ended with the stadium review on Monday, October 24. James introduced the rest of the staff and me. I really enjoyed getting recognized for stuff like that. I felt like I belonged.

On Tuesday, November 1, Liam and I went to the band banquet, a particularly long one this year. It was pretty emotional especially with Eric no longer around much. I finally got a gift from the band, a tin with cookies. (I actually still have the tin and will cherish it for many years.) I wasn't really expecting anything, but it took me a few days before I could eat the cookies, which were totally delicious.

Preparations for next year's marching band started on Tuesday, December 6, when James had a staff meeting to discuss music. Darrell and I were the only ones there for an hour until Dan and Jay finally came. We talked about doing religious music like "Amazing Grace" and "You'll Never Walk Alone." Remember how Haworth's band used to sing that song before each of our contests? I thought that was neat that we were even thinking about using it. Dan and Jay wanted Mark Barger, director at Owen Valley High School, to write our drill and let Harold write the music. It sounded good to me. However, I wouldn't be around much longer to help like I had done for the past five years. Things changed for me.

133

♫

Chapter 14

During the next three years my involvement with the Marching Artesians quickly diminished. Getting married and moving 45 minutes away, halfway between Terre Haute and Bloomington, wasn't a great thing. I still tried to be there as much as I could. I went to the first day of practice right after Liam and I got back from our honeymoon. With Liam getting home from work at about the time I needed to leave, eating supper was very quick and made me late for practice. I only missed helping with fundamentals and was there when James needed me most with the drill.

When practice resumed in July, I saw in the band office where James gave me my own mailbox. He even had my name as "Michele Fender" and even spelled Michele one "L". Finally, James could spell my name correctly! Just trying to give you a bad time, James. I felt somewhat out of it because I was late to practice, but James seemed okay with it.

During band camp a couple of weeks later, I only helped during the day so that I could be at home in the evening with Liam. I hated missing the evening stuff, but I was a newlywed and felt I needed to be at home. I didn't really do much to help except help James with errands. This was a particularly interesting year because the kids I had student taught three years ago were now freshmen. They sure gave me some funny looks.

I did get to work with the guard on a drill on Thursday. I can't believe Darrell asked me to do that. I felt funny, actually, a little nervous, doing that. I didn't really know the girls and the two boys that well. (Yes, Dan let two boys tryout.)

The day before Band Day I decided not to go see the band for morning practice thinking I would go to the Red and Blue game in the evening. However, I changed my mind about the game, too. I did call James to make sure I had a spot in the van the following day. It rained really hard for the game so I was glad I changed my mind.

Well, our big day was Wednesday, August 9, and was shortened considerably by another rainstorm. I hung out with Tracey for a while. Some former band parents were up there so I ate lunch with them. It was really hot. I thought I was going to pass out right after the kids performed. Just as we pulled away from the fairgrounds for our rest and supper, it began raining. We still managed to have our picnic at Holliday Park between raindrops until it really cut loose, and then we went to the van. James's parents were here from Pittsburgh, and I talked to them off and on. The band won the best percussion award and fifth place in the morning show. With lightning in the area and the track being really muddy, the fair officials canceled the evening performance using earlier results as final. I made it home at around midnight.

Between Band Day and the first field show competition, I didn't get to very many practices because Liam decided to become a temporary roofer and redo the one on our house. I had to be there to help out doing whatever I could, which wasn't much since I didn't know much about that kind of stuff.

Since the band's first contest was at ISU in Terre Haute on September 16, I decided not to go to Martinsville for rehearsal. It was only 45 minutes from my house to Terre Haute, a much shorter drive than the one I would have taken with the band. Instead, I called Tracey and asked if she would tell James that I would meet them there. The band didn't perform very well at all. In fact, they were seventh in their class out of eight. They only beat Bedford, who didn't make it out of district last year. Gosh, I began feeling bad. Here I was not helping as much, and the band was struggling to do well.

On Saturday, September 23, I arrived after the band had started practice and didn't really do anything to help, but at least I felt like I was part of it. I rode with James, Tracey, and Darrell to Ben Davis where we placed fourth and won best percussion. We returned to Martinsville for a supper break and a brief rehearsal. We went to Greenwood and got fourth there as well. I guess this was our fourth place day. The band was playing religious music like "Amazing Grace". Maybe the judges didn't like the music; maybe they weren't religious. Who knows? We didn't get back to Martinsville until 2 A.M. because we went to critique.

On Saturday, September 30, for the most important contest of the season, ISSMA District, I missed the first contest since becoming a staff member. Do you know how hard that was to sit at Liam's cousin's wedding wishing you were with the band?

In a bit of strangeness my mother-in-law asked Liam what time it was, and he told her 5:31 P.M., the same exact moment the band was performing. I was hoping they would do well. I guess I would find out later. I ended up calling James to find out how the band did the first part of the week and talked to Tracey. They earned a Division I.

The following Saturday I went to practice before the contest at Carmel High School. I didn't really do anything to help, and I felt bad. At least I was there even though I wasn't feeling all that great, really tired and drained. I rode to the contest with James and the Yorks. During warm-ups, we were informed the band before us, Lawrence Central, had gotten lost and had just arrived so we would perform first.

I was sitting down on the edge of the track when James walked over to me. He stood in the light so I didn't get blinded when I looked up at him. He asked me how it was possible for them to get lost, and I said they shouldn't have. He wasn't at all happy.

After the band's performance, I hung out with James and Darrell in the huge press box. They asked me if I would stay and get a recap of all the bands' scores, and I did. The band was fourth again, but they beat Warren Central and Terre Haute South. I didn't think I was going to make it home because I got so sleepy.

For the last full practice before regional, I stayed in Martinsville after subbing that day to help. I rode with James over to where the band lined up to march downtown for customer appreciation night. I still wasn't feeling all that great and didn't do much to help. Gosh, I wished that feeling would go away. However, I did torment Eric who came to help just for the evening.

"I'm studying the drill charts," he said.

"There will be a test on Saturday," I replied.

He looked at me a second and then laughed.

On Saturday, October 14, I wasn't feeling very well, but I wasn't going to miss regional in Evansville. Liam and I sat in Spencer's (Indiana) main grocery store parking lot waiting on the band to go through this small rural town. After 20 minutes of waiting, the entourage finally came through, and Liam and I grabbed a ride with George and his wife.

Well, the big moment came and went. We were seventh and about five points away from making state finals. The kids were disappointed, but in his speech James reminded them of last year and how much they had improved. George and his wife took off before the buses and dropped us off back in Spencer a little over two hours later. I had hoped we could have hung around with the band a little bit before taking off, but George wanted to get back to the school and get it opened up for the equipment truck. Liam hadn't been in band when he was in school so band didn't really interest him.

Our end-of-the-season activities happened on Tuesday, October 17, with the stadium review. I got introduced to the crowd as James always did. A band parent got the crowd to give $900 for the tractor the band wanted to buy to pull the pit equipment to and from the trucks and the football fields so the pit crew didn't have to push and pull it around.

Liam went with me to the band banquet six days later on Monday, October 23. Evidently, I didn't do enough this year because the kids didn't get me anything, which I understood.

Three days later I finally found out why I had been feeling so awful; I was avec l'enfant and about five weeks along. I was going to be a mom! No wonder I had been feeling so tired and drained. Now I would have a little marcher on the way.

For over a month I kept trying to tell James my good news, and I finally just decided to put a note in the Brennemans' Christmas card.

When I subbed one day for the high school choir director, James told me, "Congratulations."

On the Friday before spring break, four years after the last trip to Florida, the band prepared to go on another trip, and I had hoped to go. However, it hadn't worked out the way I had hoped it would. I subbed at the high school that Friday and had band kids in just about every class.

At least one of them asked me if I was going on the Florida trip, and, of course, I had to tell them, "No," as much as I wanted to say, "Yes." In fact, I was really getting tired of hearing about it because I desperately wanted to go. I hoped I didn't sub at the high school the Monday after break so I didn't have to listen to how much fun the trip was.

A couple of months later I stopped and got a 1996 marching band schedule. James sure changed things around. He wasn't doing band camp until after Band Day. I had hoped to help some that new year, but with a baby on the way I didn't know how that would work.

On May 22 I found out from Tracey when I subbed at West Middle School that a great bus driver for the band died after a two and a half year struggle with cancer. She would be missed. It sure seemed like death became a huge part of the band family. We had dealt with so much of it.

When band started right after school was out for the summer, I thought about going so James could introduce me, but I decided I was too tired and too pregnant to drive to Martinsville. Besides, I had told James I probably wouldn't be around the first couple of weeks, and he understood.

On June 29, 1996, four days after Olivia Lee was born, Mom told me she had called Brennemans and Engles. She said Tracey wasn't there, but James was writing down all of the details and repeating it back to her. I told her it was because he knew he would be in trouble if he forgot to tell her or left out details.

Once band started in July, I kept thinking and wondering how they were doing. It was driving me nuts that I couldn't be there to help. I can't tell you how hard it was for me to be sitting at home and wishing I was there. I wasn't working in the summer because I had gotten a remediation aide position at West Middle and would start in the fall. My summers were free to spend with the baby, but I did want to get out of the house some.

On Saturday, August 3, Olivia was introduced to friends in Martinsville. Mom and Dad had decided to have a small get-together since I hadn't had a baby shower for my side of the family and friends. I was really surprised to see Brennemans. They all headed for me holding and feeding Olivia when they arrived. James touched her left hand, and then he shook Dad's and Liam's hands congratulating them.

"Is the band ready for Wednesday?" I asked James.

He said, "No. Stop by sometime."

"I will," I said.

After everyone left, I made a comment to Mom and Dad about Brennemans coming and how surprised I was.

"I think you are one of James's favorites," Dad said.

He could have been right because I had taken such an interest in the band since I arrived in Martinsville 11 years before both as a member and an alumna.

On the following Tuesday, I went to Martinsville and watched the band for a little over a half hour. I forgot they practiced until noon and realized I shouldn't have gone so early. Olivia slept through what part of practice I was there. James gave the kids a break, and when he walked back out, he saw me sitting on the curb. He introduced Olivia as "the newest member of our band." I couldn't believe he did that, but I think Dad was right about what he had said Saturday. This was proof positive.

On Wednesday, August 7, I listened to Band Day on WCBK, the Martinsville radio station, during the day. The band won best color guard and percussion. I bet Dan was pretty happy. In the evening I went to bed so I didn't get to hear how well they did.

The next day the Bloomington paper said the band got fifth. I wondered how James felt about that.

That new school year I kept in contact with Tracey because I worked at West Middle. In fact, on the first day for teachers and staff, I talked to Tracey about band. She told me she had asked James if I had been to any practices. He told her he didn't expect me to be there because I had my hands full. I was glad to hear that because I was feeling really bad.

On my lunch break, I went to see James.

I told him, "I would like to help on Mondays and Wednesdays after school and maybe on Thursdays before the important contests."

He said, "That would be fine." He seemed a little surprised when I told him that.

I didn't really do much to help at the afterschool practices. In fact, I felt kind of funny being there since I hadn't been around the kids all summer. Have you ever felt like you've missed out on something when you try to join in again? Well, that was kind of the way I felt.

After the second weekend of contests, I asked Tracey at school how the band did, and she said James was pretty pleased with what they did. The percussion and color guard won awards at Ben Davis. I just wish the judges would open their eyes and really look at the creativity these kids were doing.

The only contest I went with the band was to district at Columbus East. I left Olivia with Mom and Dad and enjoyed the day as I wanted. The band received a Division I. That was nice that I got to spend the day away from Olivia and spend time with the band I loved.

The following week I thought about taking Olivia and going to Center Grove since it was close and during the day, but the weather wasn't all that great, kind of chilly, and I didn't think an almost 4-month-old baby needed to be out in that.

The following week I tried to figure out a way I could go with the band to regional. I heard the weather was supposed to be really cold, and since the band didn't perform until almost last, I doubted that I would go. I thought about the band as they practiced on Thursday before the big day. Something told me they wouldn't be marching in the Hoosier Dome this year; I still called it that even though it had been renamed the RCA Dome.

On Saturday I thought about the band all day long, wishing I could be there to cheer them on. I didn't do my letter to the editor like I usually did. I just didn't think it would do much good at this point. I did look at what the yearbook, *The Martinsville Reporter,* did again for the band. Of course, my picture wasn't in it, and I felt bad about that because I really missed helping them.

The stadium review and band banquet took place a couple of weeks later. I really wanted to go and show off Olivia, but that didn't work out either time. I really did miss being able to help with the band that year. I felt like an outcast when I was around them even though James tried hard to make me feel like I was still a part of them. I really appreciated what he tried to do for me.

If you thought I really slacked off in 1996, wait until you see 1997. I don't have many details so I'm relying on my mind to recall them. Then again I basically stopped helping the band all together. In other words, there's not much to tell.

By the time practices started in July, Olivia walked pretty well. I decided to stay in Martinsville for an evening practice. The staff and the kids got a kick out of watching her walking up and down the sideline. At one point she started walking out across the parking lot toward the kids who were practicing fundamentals a good distance away from us.

As Olivia walked away, James said, "She marches better than some of the bigger kids."

Later that same evening, Olivia and I went to talk to James in his office about me getting a T-shirt and helping with band more this year. He did pay for a shirt and told me he could always use an extra set of eyes. I left before the end of practice.

I didn't get back to help until the two days before Band Day when they had rehearsal in the morning. I spent the first day chasing Olivia up and down the sideline. Now that she could walk that was all she wanted to do.

On the second day I left her with my grandma. During those two days I tried to figure out a way to go to Band Day because it was only supposed to be around 74 degrees, a beautiful day. My grandma and even Mom offered to go, but I decided it would make a long day for Olivia.

I tried to go to as many after school practices as I could. I did even manage to make it to a couple of contests, one with and one without Olivia. Kathy, the orchestra director at the high school, whose daughter Sydney was a week older than Olivia, and I decided to take the girls to their first band contest at the Columbus East Invitational. They didn't do too badly until Olivia decided she was ready for a nap about halfway through the band's show and fell asleep on my lap. Up until then, though, the band did seem to interest her. She sure paid attention to the other bands on the field.

My last memory of this particular marching band season was attending regional at Jeffersonville, moved from Evansville. I left Olivia once again with Mom and Dad and rode with Brennemans and Darrell. I felt really lost because I only knew about half of the band. The kids I had student taught were now juniors. It was just a really weird day for me because I was really beginning to feel like a total outcast. At this point I made up my mind that I wanted to help more next year. I had to be there when those juniors became seniors.

At this point that's where I am with my memories, not really a good ending, huh? How can I end something like this as long as James is still director and I am still associating myself with the band? I continued getting myself pumped for helping with the band and even told Tracey that was what I planned on doing.

♫

Epilogue

Well, I now have more of an ending to what I've shared with you so far. In June 1998 Kathy told me that James got a job at Bedford Junior High School. I couldn't say anything. So many thoughts went racing through my mind. Would the Brennemans move down there, especially since Tracey's parents lived there? Would I still help with the band? Once the questions stopped racing around, I realized that I wasn't thinking straight. This job was what James had been wanting for four years. I should be happy for him. Who was I kidding? Kathy also told me Dan wouldn't be helping as much. Maybe this was my sign that I didn't need to be helping with band anymore, that I had a two-year-old to take care of.

Besides, if I was worried about staying in contact with the Brennemans, I still had Tracey to talk to at school. I couldn't stop thinking about this. I thought about going ahead and helping, but then a few weeks later I found out Darrell was leaving, too, for Plainfield. At that moment I decided my staff days were over. I didn't want to help a band where I didn't know the staff and didn't even know if the new director would even want my help. This wasn't the way I wanted this to end. I felt like I had let James down by not being there those last couple of years, but I think he understood.

Once the new school year started, I talked to Tracey. They had put their house up for sale and were looking at a house just inside the Lawrence County line toward Bedford. She said James had three or four schools, Bedford Junior High, Oolitic Junior High, and one or two elementaries, to drive to each day, but no marching band, no bunches of times away from his family.

Some of the band members decided to put together an open house to honor James for his many years of service with the band. I knew I had to go when I heard about it, and, of course, Ashley had to go. I decided to buy him a card, one with Mickey Mouse on the front, an appropriate one I thought since I had gone to Disney World with the band.

As I finish writing this book, so many memories have come back, memories that I will never forget and memories that I shouldn't share because of the personal meaning to me and things that shouldn't be shared because they have nothing to do with what marching band is all about, but rather relate to my life. Marching band was such an important part of my life. I don't know what I would have done without it both as a student and as an adult. As a student, my family moved to three locations, and band helped me meet others and gave me an extra-curricular activity. As an adult, marching band was my social life and my way of figuring out what I wanted to do with my life, to become a teacher. It also gained me friends that I will never forget even if I no longer keep in touch.

So many things happened during my 11-year association with the Martinsville Marching Artesians that I couldn't begin to write it all down. I still don't really consider myself completely gone even though James is. Instead, I've written the highlights, the memories that I remember or cherish the most, the memories that made me laugh and/or cry. I wish I could relive these memories, but that's not possible.

Printed in the United States
39362LVS00007B/11